UNTIL
THE WHISTLE
BLOWS

GOODYEAR EDUCATION SERIES

Change for Children
Sandra N. Kaplan, Jo Ann B. Kaplan, Sheila K. Madsen, Bette K. Taylor

Creating a Learning Environment
Ethel Breyfogle, Pamela Santich, Ronald Kremer, Susan Nelson, Carol Pitts

Do You Read Me?
Arnold Griese

Imagine That!
Joyce King and Carol Katzman

The Language Arts Idea Book
Joanne D. Schaff

The Learning Center Book
Tom Davidson, Phyllis Fountain, Rachel Grogan, Verl Short, Judy Steely, Katherine Freeman

Loving and Beyond
Joe Abruscato and Jack Hassard

Mainstreaming Language Arts and Social Studies
Charles R. Coble, Anne Adams, Paul B. Hounshell

Mainstreaming Science and Math
Charles R. Coble, Anne Adams, Paul B. Hounshell

New Schools for a New Age
William Georgiades, Reuben Hilde, Grant Macaulay

One at a Time All at Once
Jack E. Blackburn and Conrad Powell

The Other Side of the Report Card
Larry Chase

An Ounce of Prevention Plus a Pound of Cure
Ronald W. Bruton

Reaching Teenagers
Don Beach

The Reading Corner
Harry W. Forgan

A Survival Kit for Teachers and Parents
Myrtle T. Collins and DWane R. Collins

The Whole Cosmos Catalog of Science Activities
Joe Abruscato and Jack Hassard

**Will the Real Teacher Please Stand Up?
Second edition**
Mary C. Greer and Bonnie Rubinstein

A Young Child Experiences
Sandra N. Kaplan, Jo Ann B. Kaplan, Sheila K. Madsen, Bette K. Gould

UNTIL THE WHISTLE BLOWS

A Collection of Games, Dances, and Activities for Eight- to Twelve-Year-olds

J. Tillman Hall, Ed.D.
Nancy Hall Sweeny
Jody Hall Esser

Goodyear Publishing Company, Inc.
Santa Monica, California

Library of Congress Cataloging in Publication Data
Hall, J. Tillman.
    Until the whistle blows: a collection of games,
dances and activities for eight to twelve year olds.

    (Goodyear education series)
    Bibliography: p.
    Includes index.
    1.   Perceptual-motor learning.   2.   Educational games.
I.   Sweeny, Nancy Hall, joint author.   II.   Esser, Jody Hall,
joint author.   III.   Title.
LB1067.H26   372.1'3   76-55311
ISBN 0-87620-919-3

Library of Congress Catalog Card Number: 76-55311
ISBN: 0-87620-919-3
Y-9193-7
Current Printing (last number):
10 9 8 7 6 5 4 3 2 1

Sherri Butterfield, project editor
Louie Neiheisel, designer and art director
Kitty Anderson, illustrator
Thompson Type, typographer

Printed in the United States of America

ABOUT THIS BOOK

This book is based on the assumption that you—as a parent, youth leader, camp counselor, or teacher—supervise children's play. It is designed to make the task easier for you and the play more meaningful for the children. It is about the proper selection of physical activities for children aged eight to twelve to provide enjoyment and exercise and to develop physical fitness, positive self-image, sound social behavior, and recreational interest.

PHILOSOPHY

Because life is brief, with much to be learned, it is imperative that all children be given a head start in learning about themselves and their environment. Many reach maturity and are limited in their achievements because they failed to develop specific abilities while they were young. It is extremely important that children between the ages of four and twelve be given maximum help in overcoming deficiencies in motor coordination, in social skills, and in the development of their intellectual capabilities. Many children have a variety of gross and fine motor problems, such as poor coordination, general awkwardness, and defective perceptual acuity. Most of these problems could be arrested or even eliminated through directed play or participation in effective activity and recreation programs. To help you guide children in such play or develop and implement an innovative activity program for your youth group, campers, or class is the purpose of this book.

CONTENTS

This book is divided into nine chapters. Chapters 1 and 2 discuss the physical, emotional, and intellectual needs of children and how some of these needs can be met, correct basic movement patterns established, and desirable skills developed through a formal movement education program, or through less formal activity periods. These two chapters emphasize the importance of identifying your objectives—whether you desire to entertain the children at Jennifer's birthday party, help Michael learn to read by improving his balance, fill a 45-minute period in the campers' day, give the Scouts a chance to blow off steam before settling down to business at their Monday afternoon meeting, develop a ball team, or fill the time until the whistle blows ending the play period.

Chapters 3, 4, 5, 6, 7, and 8 detail, in words, pictures, and diagrams, over 150 games, dances, and activities with special emphasis on team sports and such programs as nature study, camping, and crafts. Within each chapter, the activities are arranged from simple to complex and are grouped according to difficulty level. You may need to try portions of several activities to determine where to begin; skill evaluation forms will help you decide when the children are ready to progress to the next difficulty level.

Included in Chapter 4 is a **dance description chart** listing all the dances in the chapter and showing for each the country of origin, the degree of difficulty for eight- to twelve-year-olds, the basic steps, and the page on which the directions for the dance appear. Detailed dance directions include not only the basic steps, formation, and step-by-step instructions, but also a list of records that can be used for the dance. At the end of the chapter is a **list of record sources** containing the names and mailing addresses—categorized by geographical area—of companies from which these records can be obtained.

In addition to detailed skill development instructions for team sports, Chapter 7 includes **reproducible score sheets, tournament diagrams**, an **injury report form**, and a **leader's self-evaluation checklist**.

So that you may combine these activities in any way you feel is beneficial, they have ordinarily been printed one to a page. Should you wish to locate a specific game or dance, or activities in which a particular piece of equipment (e.g., ball) is used or a specific skill is developed, consult either the **index of activities and terms** or the **index of skills**, both located at the back of the book.

Chapter 9, entitled "The Building Blocks of Physical Life," is an illustrated discussion of the human body and how it knows, grows, and goes. Included are brief descriptions of the skeletal, muscular, cardiovascular, lymphatic, respiratory, nervous, digestive, and endocrine systems, with emphasis upon how these systems affect and/or are affected by exercise, posture, nutrition, and disease or infection. The full-page line drawings in this chapter are designed to be used as is, shown on a screen by means of an opaque projector, or reproduced by making a thermofax master and using a ditto machine to run off the number of copies needed for your group or class. A section on safety and accident prevention concludes this chapter.

FORMAT AND FEATURES

The pages in this book are of **standard notebook size** (8½″ x 11″) to give maximum space for explanations, illustrations, and your notes or observations. The **extra large type** used for the activity descriptions enables you to read and understand them at a glance. The book has been **three-hole punched** so that individual pages or the entire book can be easily stored and used as part of your meeting, lesson, or activity plan notebook, and arranged or rearranged in any order you choose.

The **evaluation sheets** throughout the book, the **score sheets** in Chapter 7, and the **anatomical illustrations** in Chapter 9 have been designed to be reproduced. Sheets intended for reproduction, as well as the individual activity sheets, have been marked with **printed cut lines**.

So that you can easily find the activity you need, the brief **back cover contents list** has been arrow referenced to the **chapter number flip indexing** within.

A special feature of this book is the **four-color poster**. Intended to be both decorative and informative, it shows the major muscles of the body and the antigravity muscles, those that work together to combat the pull of gravity and make standing upright possible.

POSTSCRIPT

Should these activities seem inappropriate for your children, look into the companion volume to this one (magenta cover). Written by the same authors for four- to eight-year-olds, it not only describes easier variations on some of these same activities, but also includes finger plays, let's pretend activities, and a special chapter on perceptual-motor learning.

OUR THANKS TO . . .

Amy, Anne, Brian, Jean, John, Kent, Kirsten, Michelle, Nick, Tara, and Trevor, who helped Kitty create the illustrations.

Paul Tickenoff, who allowed us to use the Mission Viejo Gymnastic Center.

Bill Call, who took the photographs.

Norman H. Rossell, assistant superintendent, Los Angeles City Unified School District, who gave us permission to use drill charts from *Physical Education Teaching Guide, Grades Three, Four, Five, Six* (Division of Instructional Services, Publication No. EC-537, 1961) as "models" for some of the drawings in Chapter 7.

Bobbye Jean Hammond, who typed the final manuscript.

Alice Harmon, Cher Threinen, and Bobbye Jean Hammond, who helped put the book together.

Shirley Coleman and Bob Thompson, whose accurate typesetting and excellent advice made the task much easier.

ABOUT THESE AUTHORS

J. Tillman Hall and his two talented daughters have had extensive experience in teaching children, in traveling with groups of youngsters, and in observing them at play in many parts of the world.

Dr. Hall grew up in a small rural community in West Tennessee. His childhood experiences included many of the recreational activities that interest children everywhere. He excelled in varsity sports in both high school and college, and was active in a variety of school activities, including dramatics, singing and musical groups, social clubs, and intramural games.

After graduation Dr. Hall began his professional career as principal of the elementary school and head coach of all sports at Big Sandy, Tennessee, high school. He served five years in the Navy during World War II, and became coach and head of the Physical Education Department at George Pepperdine College (now Pepperdine University) upon his return from active duty. After earning his doctorate, he was named professor and head of the Physical Education Department at the University of Southern California, the position he currently holds.

He is in the process of writing his ninth textbook, has edited twenty-three books, and has received numerous commendations for his contributions to the education of children from such organizations as the Parent-Teachers' Association, *McCall's*, the City of Los Angeles, Los Angeles County, the California State Legislature, Culver City, California Governor Ronald Reagan, and the Southwest District American Alliance for Health, Physical Education, and Recreation (AAHPER). He is a recipient of the coveted National AAHPER Honor Award and is listed in *Who's Who in the United States*.

Nancy graduated from the University of Southern California (USC) and has done graduate work at USC, California State University at Fresno, and Pepperdine University. She has danced on various television programs and has made stage appearances throughout the fifty states. Her first teaching positions were in Los Angeles and Fresno, California. Later she became head of the primary physical education program for Pilgrim School, a private school for gifted children. She is currently teaching art at Pilgrim School and creative rhythms and outdoor education at the University of Southern California. She is married to Culver City Fire Chief George Sweeny and has two children, six-year-old Brian and nine-year-old Michelle.

Jody graduated from the University of Southern California and has done graduate work at California State University at Northridge (CSUN). She has had extensive experience on stage and in television as both a performer and a choreographer with children and adults. Having taught at CSUN and at Santa Monica City College, she is currently teaching specialized courses in dance and gymnastics and recreation at the University of Southern California. She is married to Jack Esser, a defense systems analyst with Research and Development Associates (RDA).

JODY   DR. HALL   NANCY

CONTENTS

1. CHILDREN'S NEEDS AND HOW THIS BOOK CAN HELP YOU MEET THEM . . . .

Primary Needs **1**
Secondary Needs **1**
Educational Needs **2**

Learning **3**
Cognitive Skills **3**
Behavioral Skills **3**

Movement Skills **3**
Your Role **4**
Conclusion **7**

2. PRINCIPLES AND OBJECTIVES OF MOVEMENT EDUCATION . . . .

Principles **9**
Objectives **10**

Basic Movements **11**

Upside-Down and Inside-Ou[

3. CREATIVE MOVEMENT . . . .

Balancing Activities **14**
Walking Activities **15**
Making a Straw Horn **16**
Running Activities **17**
Hopping Activities **18**
Skipping Activities **19**
Stretching Activities **20**

Twisting Activities **21**
Swinging and Turning
   Activities **22**
Lifting Activities **23**
Hoop Activities **24**
Parachute Activities **25**

Rope Activities 1 **26**
Rope Activities 2 **27**
Rope Activities 3 **28**
Rope Activities 4 **29**
Rope Activities 5 **30-31**
Beanbag Activities **32**
Relaxing Activities **33**

4. RHYTHMS AND DANCE . . . .

Elements of Rhythm **35**
Terms **36**
Basic Formations **37-38**
Positions **39-40**
Dance Description Chart **41**
Hora **42**
All-American Promenade **43**
Double Clap Polka **44**
Kentwood Schottische **45**
Patty-cake Polka **46**
Virginia Reel **47-48**
Evaluation **49**

Alunelul **50**
Put Your Little Foot **51-52**
Lili Marlene **53**
Oxdansen **54-55**
Lummi Stick Dance **56-57**
Teton Mountain Stomp **58**
Scottish Sword Dance **59-60**
Evaluation **61**
Gathering Peasecods **62-63**
The Two-Step **64-65**
Tea for Two **66**
The Waltz **67-68**

Rye Waltz **69**
Hot Time **70**
Additional Square Dances **7**
Grand Square **72-73**
Tinikling **74-75**
Old Dobbin **76-77**
Evaluation **78**
Other Dances Suggested for
   Level **78**
Record Sources **79**

5. STUNTS AND TUMBLING . . . .

Warm-up Activities **82-84**
Crane Dive **85**
Balance and Reverse **86**
Coffee Grinder **87**
Falling **88**
Forward Roll **89-90**
Human Ball **91**
Bicycling **92**
Up and Over **93**
Tripod Tip-up **94**
Jump from Knees **95**
Backward Roll **96**
Partner Hop **97**
Balance Beam Activities **98**

Evaluation **99**
Warm-up Activities **100-101**
Tripod Headstand **102**
Headstand Kick-up **103**
Double Forward Roll **104**
Russian Dance **105**
Skin the Snake **106**
Dive Roll **107**
Partner Handstand **108**
Handstand **109**
Monkey Roll **110**
Six-Legged Animal **111**
Rooster Fight **112**
Evaluation **113**

Warm-up Activities **114-116**
The Bridge **117**
Base of Support **118**
Turnover **119**
Push and Clap **120**
Merry-Go-Round **121**
One-Arm Wrestle **122**
Backward Extension Roll **12**
Forward to Backward Roll **1**
Balance Beam Routine **125**
Cartwheel **126**
Evaluation **127**

6. GAMES 129

Dress-up Relay **130-131**
Dodge Ball **132**
Rock, Paper, Scissors **133**
Newspaper Relay **134**
Hangman **135**
Streets and Alleys **136**

Four Square **137**
Box Ball **138**
Chain Tag **139**
Crown the King **140**
Jump the Shot **141**
Ball and Stick Relay **142**

Team Dodge Ball **143**
Find a Place **144**
Hindu Tag **145**
Keep Away **146**
Rescue Relay **147**

7. TEAM SPORTS 149

Soccer **150-153**
Flag Football **154-157**
Volleyball **158-160**
Volleyball Score Sheet **161**
Basketball **162-164**
Basketball Score Sheet **165**
Softball **166-168**
Softball Score Sheet **169**

Tournaments **170-171**
Ladder Tournament Form **172**
Pyramid Tournament Form **173**
Elimination Tournament
    Form **174**
Round Robin Tournament
    Organization **175**
Forms **176**

Track and Field Master Score
    Sheet **177**
Percentage Table **178**
Injury Report **179**
Leadership Evaluation **180**
Leader's Self-Evaluation
    Checklist **181**

8. SPECIAL PROGRAMS 183

Nature Study **183**
Camping **184**
Crafts **184**

Pasta Painting **185**
Decorative Hanging or
    Banner **186**

Shell Boat **186**
Nutty Animals **187**

9. THE BUILDING BLOCKS OF PHYSICAL LIFE 189

The Human Cell **189-190**
Systems **191**
The Skeletal System **192-193**
The Muscular System **194-195**
Posture **196-197**
The Cardiovascular
    System **198-199**

The Lymphatic System **200-201**
The Endocrine System **202-203**
The Respiratory System **204-205**
The Nervous System **206-207**
The Digestive System **208-209**
Nutrition **210**

The Body's Vitamin and Mineral
    Needs **211**
Diseases **212**
The Body's Defenses **212**
Safety and Accident
    Prevention **213**
Conclusion **213**

BIBLIOGRAPHY 215

INDEX OF ACTIVITIES AND TERMS 217-222

INDEX OF SKILLS 223

CHILDREN'S NEEDS AND HOW THIS BOOK CAN HELP YOU MEET THEM

1.

Parents, teachers, group leaders, camp counselors—all who work with children must, to some extent, meet the needs of those children, or recognize with regret that they have failed at their task. Some needs do not have to be identified to be met. A certain amount of need satisfaction occurs naturally, unconsciously: children seek out trees to climb without being told, and adults cheer their successes and wipe away their tears without being taught. Other needs, in going unnoticed, also go unmet. Before trying to satisfy them, one must know what they are. One must ask: Exactly, what are the needs of children?

PRIMARY NEEDS

Basic to life itself are food, drink, air, rest, and sleep. These primary needs are somewhat the same for everyone. The amount required may vary, depending on such factors as maturity, physiological efficiency, and intensity of activity; but unless these needs are adequately met, the organism cannot function properly.

SECONDARY NEEDS

Children have a large number of secondary needs, and the degree to which these needs are satisfied often determines how well they adjust to the society in which they live. Fifteen that seem most essential are listed below, with recommendations for meeting them.

1. To acquire knowledge. Children have a desire to learn new truths. They are inquisitive and ask countless questions. This searching, questioning attitude is fundamental to building wisdom. One way to teach children is to direct their natural inquisitiveness with carefully considered questions: Wooden bats are made from what kind of tree? Where does this type of tree grow? How fast does a tree grow? In what city are most bats manufactured? What is a bone? How does it develop? What must I eat to improve bone growth? How many bones does a child have? An

adult? What is the purpose of bones? How does the skeleton of a man differ from that of an animal, or an insect? Can bones move by themselves? The answers can be discovered in dictionaries, almanacs, encyclopedias, and other reference books, in school and community libraries, and by "asking the experts."

2. To be creative. Children have a desire to play, to make believe, to build something based upon their own imagination. Rhythm, craft, and drama activities provide creative experiences and aid in developing a "can do" attitude.

3. To belong to a group. Children are gregarious and have a desire to become affiliated with various groups. They like to belong, respond to, be responded to, and be recognized. The group and team activities in this book satisfy this secondary need, "belongingness."

4. To be adventurous. Children have a burning desire to see what is on the other side of the mountain. New experiences, if rewarding, encourage further exploration. Outdoor education, nature study, puzzles, craft classes, and other activities that require some physical skills along with strategic maneuvering help satisfy this secondary need.

5. To be active. The typical child cannot be still very long. It seems as if each cell in his body desires and thrives on exercise. The games and activities in this book will satisfy his present activity needs while developing the muscle tone and coordination required to meet future needs.

6. To be competitive. Most American children are aggressive and desire to match their skills and strategies against those of other children. Properly directed physical activities afford one of the best opportunities to satisfy this need.

7. To be loved. The prepossessing child desires to love and to be loved, to feel wanted, needed, and welcomed. Being included as a necessary member of a group or team in the activities described in this book helps satisfy his need to feel essential.

8. To be successful. Like grown-ups, children desire to be successful. Most of them strive to excell, to be the best, to achieve the most, for which they like to be complimented or rewarded. It is as meaningful for a young child to be awarded a certificate or ribbon for his efforts as it is for an older boy or girl to receive a trophy, sweater, or plaque. Physical activities afford innumerable opportunities for successful experiences, especially if rewards and recognition are liberally given.

9. To feel secure. Children desire to feel safe and to be protected. Games played according to well-defined rules create a feeling of security and build respect for justice and fair play. Meaningful rules that assure good sportsmanship are an American tradition.

10. To manipulate objects. Children have a strong drive to feel and touch objects and to move them from one place to another. This desire can be partly satisfied in playing darts, checkers, chess, and various ball games, and in nature study.

11. To express oneself. Children desire to express themselves vocally, skillfully, rhythmically. Such activities as dance, rhythmic movement, speech, and dramatics afford them an opportunity to do so.

12. To be self-actualized. Self-actualization is a gratifying experience. One progresses toward self-actualization as he strives to realize his full potential, adjusting his goals as the result of learning and motivation. Self-actualization happens when he believes in the adequacy of his learning and in the validity of his value system. A moment of truth occurs during competition when a runner realizes he gave his all but lost to a better performer. He learns to recognize the limits of his ability and to set more realistic goals

for himself—or to work harder. Participation in competitive physical activities fosters self-actualization.

13. To be contented. Children have an intense desire to be happy. Their activities should be gratifying, should provide numerous opportunities for pleasure.

14. To be attractive. Children desire to be captivating. To achieve this goal, they must make use of a number of personal qualities, such as cleanliness and hygiene, proper dress and grooming, good posture and physical fitness, personality and their ability to communicate. Well-organized physical activities and recreation programs can develop these qualities.

15. To be physically skilled. Most children desire to participate in various physical activities. Activity skill classes can aid in developing fundamental movement patterns. If motivated to practice, children who have potential may become highly skilled performers.

EDUCATIONAL NEEDS

From time to time agents of a society attempt to identify and list abilities, attitudes, and other forms of behavior which seem to have a positive value in that society. These are then presented in a controlled environment, such as a school, in an attempt to aid children in attaining social competence and optimum development. Perhaps the premier such list was that of the Seven Cardinal Aims of Education:

1. Health
2. Worthy home membership
3. Command of the fundamental processes
4. Vocational training
5. Worthy use of leisure time
6. Citizenship
7. Ethical character

These goals cover the whole of education—and of life itself.

The Educational Policies Commission reduced these aims to the following four fundamental concepts:

1. Self-realization. This process would include developing (1) an inquiring mind; (2) improved skills in speaking, reading, and writing; (3) knowledge of health and disease; (4) improved physical and mental health; (5) skill in participant sports; (6) knowledge of spectator sports; (7) worthy use of leisure time; and (8) aesthetic skills and appreciations.

2. Human relationships. This area encompasses the development of superior human relations, understanding, and appreciation through cooperative play, and would also include courtesy, fair play, and good sportsmanship.

3. Economic efficiency. The aim here is to develop the skills of, an understanding of, and a respect for both the vocational and the consumer aspects of living.

4. Civic responsibility. This concept includes continued growth in understanding and practicing humanitarianism, tolerance, and conservation, in conforming to the law, and in appreciating democratic living.

LEARNING

Learning is generally defined as a change in response or behavior involving some degree of permanence. It results from gaining new knowledge, developing new insights, and/or establishing new skills through the media of study and experience. It is the process by which an idea or activity originates or is changed through experience rather than by growth, development, and maturation.

Learning includes all sorts of changes, such as acquiring a vocabulary, operating a typewriter, and developing prejudices, preferences, social attitudes, and ideals. It tends to improve with practice. Furthermore, it is not necessary to master technical knowledge about the cerebrospinal aspects of learning to know when learning occurs: if something has been learned, it can be repeated, and it is usually measurable.

The speed at which one learns new skills usually depends upon previous learning and experiences, interest in the task to be learned, and maturation. Because children seldom assimilate with permanency more than they understand, it may be necessary to adapt the learning task—activities, games, and the rules by which they are ordinarily played—to their ability level, and perhaps to make a whole game of a single part of an activity.

Regardless of what educational needs one lists and of how learning takes place—and there are nearly as many theories about that as there are people to write about them—the primary purpose of our teaching should be to aid children in developing the skills essential to the accomplishment of present and future tasks. These skills can be classified as cognitive, behavioral, or movement skills.

COGNITIVE SKILLS

Cognition includes all of the intellectual activities as distinguished from conation and affection. It is the mental process by which knowledge, perception, and reasoning occur or are acquired.

BEHAVIORAL SKILLS

Knowledge is regarded as a necessity for wise self-direction, but education should be considered more than the mastery of knowledge: it also includes changes in one's behavior. Such changes may be based on concomitant affective learning, that is, changes in attitudes. Changing attitudes in a multicultural society such as ours may be controversial, but the challenge to do so must not go unmet.

Behavioral skills to be mastered include not only those governing one's relationship with other individuals, but also those essential to one's personal development, such as good study and eating habits, proper exercise, and relaxation techniques.

MOVEMENT SKILLS

Movement skills are learned movement patterns essential to the development of physical efficiency. In their teaching should be reflected the development of the total human movement potential. It takes a baby many months, even with highly individualized tutoring, to learn to roll over, sit up, crawl, pull up, stand, walk, climb, and feed himself. The same kind of guidance and encouragement would be most beneficial in teaching complicated movement patterns to children of elementary school age.

Physical activity periods should be much more than an aimless expenditure of energy or an escape from boredom. As movement or activity education periods, they should be directed, whenever possible, toward the development of desired physical, social, and mental skills, and should encompass activities characterized by

1

maximal enjoyment, good physical exercise, and efficient movement patterns.

Your activity program should include movement skills in each of the following categories:

1. Skills of locomotion
   - Walking correctly (tall, toes straight ahead, one foot always touching the ground)
   - Running (upright, bent over, backward, fast, slow, with both feet off the ground)
   - Jumping (take off on both feet at the same time)
   - Hopping (first on the left foot several times, then on the right foot)
   - Sliding (moving sideways)
   - Skipping (step-hop, first on one foot, then on the other)
   - Leaping (take off on one foot and land on the other)
   - Galloping (One foot reaches in leaping motion. As the other foot is brought up to the lead foot, weight is shifted to it from the lead foot in a short hopping motion. The sequence is repeated rapidly with the same foot leading.)
2. Skills used in assuming a fixed position
   - Lying
   - Sitting
   - Kneeling
   - Squatting
   - Standing
   - Hanging
3. Skills used in playing games and sports
   - Starting
   - Pivoting
   - Stopping
   - Dodging
   - Catching
   - Striking
   - Batting
   - Dribbling
   - Kicking
   - Balancing
   - Vaulting
   - Eye-body coordination

YOUR ROLE

Your role in selecting and teaching physical activities includes defining objectives; organizing materials and equipment; testing, evaluating, and prescribing activities for children; and motivating them to participate and to learn.

Defining Objectives

It has been said that there is no teaching unless some learning takes place. You should have planned objectives and should strive for both general and specific outcomes without excluding the joyful ingredient found in children's play: purposeful activity can be playful.

In 1973 the California State Board of Education adopted a rather comprehensive set of guidelines for physical education. Apparently based on the Seven Cardinal Aims of Education and on the recommendations of the Educational Policies Commission, they differ in that they specifically identify the needs and objectives of physical education. Those that seem relevant for four- to twelve-year-olds are:

1. Basic movement skills should be taught in games and relays in both individual and dual sports, stunts and tumbling, physical fitness activities, rhythmic and dance activities, and team sports.

2. In selecting and teaching physical activities, consideration should be given to cultural needs, including both similarities and differences. When specific activities are repulsive to a given community, they should probably not be included in the program.

3. Whenever possible, time should be devoted to improving physical fitness through vigorous activity. (In fact, every able-bodied individual should exercise vigorously, to the point of raising his heartbeat to 125 beats per minute, for at least four minutes each day. He can do so by jogging, running, cycling, or performing various kinds of calesthenics. Maintaining a strong cardiovascular system depends on this kind of exercise.)

4. Physical activity periods should be organized to encourage maximum participation. Enough suitable equipment for practicing specific skills should be made available so that children do not have to wait their turn. Time spent standing in line is wasted and tends to diminish the interest children normally have in being active. All children in the group should be throwing, catching, tossing, running, jumping, dancing, or climbing at the same time—not watching and waiting.

5. Children need instruction in how to develop and improve the following skills:

- Posture—sitting, standing, and moving
- Eye-hand, eye-foot, and eye-body coordination
- Preferred hand and foot, along with bilateral movements
- Awareness of spatial relationships
- Creative expression, self-direction, and independent exploration
- Positive image of self and others
- Appreciation of others in play, work, and study
- Leadership in choosing, demonstrating, and assisting others
- Safety in both work and play
- Understanding the body and how it functions
- Developing and maintaining physical fitness
- Selecting recreational activities that contribute to the worthy use of leisure time
- Foreseeing the consequences of one's actions
- Basic body mechanics for lifting, pulling, pushing, carrying, and supporting various objects

In summary, your physical education or recreation program should include a variety of activities to develop motor skills, physical fitness, self-image, social behavior, and recreational interest.

Teaching activities in sequence according to their difficulty will make it possible for each child to begin at his own proficiency level and progress logically, building each new achievement upon the mastery of its prerequisite skill or skills. The materials in each chapter of this book are arranged in sequential order from simple to complex movement patterns. An occasional review of various recommended activities will often help children perfect movement patterns.

Proficiency in executing movement skills depends on the intensity and frequency of supervised practice sessions. Specific attention should be given to teaching correct movement patterns: ineffective movements, once they have become habitual, are difficult to change.

Keep in mind that, as a child grows, his strength, stamina, coordination, and fine motor skills may vary. He must make a number of complicated adjustments to compensate for relatively small changes in height and weight if he is to repeat certain movements with the same efficiency. Rapid increases in leg length and body weight often result in awkwardness. Special compassion and understanding are needed when this occurs. Children who understand the somewhat mysterious process of growth and development should progress more readily than those who do not and should have greater tolerance for those who seem to move less efficiently; therefore, we encourage you to teach and have the children read about how the body grows, develops, and works, and have included a chapter on this subject at the end of the book.

1

Testing and Evaluating

The extensive use of intelligence, aptitude, and achievement tests may be permanently and adversely affecting the lives and attitudes of many children. Branded as "nonachievers" because of poor test performance, they come to believe they really are inferior to those making higher scores. This is not right, and we know it! Children are more like one another than they are different: the variability is one of degree rather than one of kind. Test scores and evaluations should be used for diagnostic purposes, to determine a child's proficiency level or areas of weakness so that sufficiently challenging or remedial activities can be prescribed, never as a tool to stagnate anyone at any particular level of physical development.

Stimulating and Motivating

Playtime should not be wasted time. In this complex world, there is so much one needs to know that children should not be permitted to learn everything through haphazard personal discov-

ery. Every effort should be made to stimulate each child, to increase his understanding of himself and of the world in which he lives. Successful change entails growth and development. Each child should be encouraged to take part in mind-stretching and body-developing exercises and experiences.

When one participates in an activity, learning is not automatic. There is a definite relationship, however, between the amount one learns and the interest one has in what he is doing. For this reason, considerable effort should be directed toward stimulating eagerness for activities that seem most worthwhile.

One way to motivate interest in physical fitness and skill development is through self-testing. Post score sheets on bulletin boards and have children record the number of times they can repeat an exercise before tiring or making a mistake, the distance jumped, the time in which a specified distance was run, and so forth. Rather than being pitted one against another, the children can be encouraged to better their own scores of yesterday or last week. The following physical skills lend themselves to self-testing:

1. Individual rope jumping (number of times)
2. Sit-ups (number)
3. Push-ups (number)
4. Running (distance, time)
5. Dribbling a ball (with left hand, with right hand, alternating hands)
6. Throwing balls for accuracy and distance
7. Balancing
   - on one leg or the other
   - on the balance beam
   - with a book on the head
   - on a skate board
   - on roller skates
   - on ice skates
   - on a bicycle
8. Jumping (distance, height)
9. Volleying
   - against a backboard
   - in table tennis
   - in tennis
10. Shooting balls through hoops (basketball)

Many other activities can be used for self-testing: this list offers only a brief sample. Given this challenge, children seem to enjoy seeing how many times they can successfully repeat an exercise, and repetition of movements tends to improve their performance.

CONCLUSION

Our complex world presents each new occupant with a plethora of stimuli and of challenges. To make sense of the stimuli and to meet the challenges, children must master many cognitive, behavioral, and movement skills; develop and control a number of personal qualities; and alter certain ideas and attitudes. In addition, they have certain needs that must be met, in part, by the society in which they find themselves. A well-designed movement education program can go a long way toward developing the required skills, qualities, and attitudes, and toward meeting many secondary needs. This book outlines such a program. The activities in it are vehicles through which countless concomitant learnings may take place. Your challenge lies in selecting specific activities to meet recognized needs and in presenting them in a manner that motivates children to participate, learn, and develop.

PRINCIPLES AND OBJECTIVES OF MOVEMENT EDUCATION

2.

We have said that a variety of needs can be met and desirable skills developed through a formal movement education program, or through less formal activity periods. Courtesy, fair play, and good sportsmanship can best be learned as a participant in supervised play activities, and participation in such activities enhances a child's ability to make correct judgments.

A large collection of little experiences enriches a child's total experience, and there is practically no end to the activity experiences available to children. Among the possibilities are:

- Playground activities
- Outdoor education projects
- Field trips
- Dramatics
- Arts and crafts
- Camping
- Music, singing, and band activities
- Before and after school activities
- Recess and noontime activities
- Weekend and vacation time experiences
- Club activities
- Individual and team sports

The time and activities are available. What is needed is someone to plan and direct these experiences.

If you are that someone, you will need to consider the principles on which your program will be based and to identify your objectives. Without them, your movement education program or activity period will be haphazard—doomed to mediocrity, or even failure.

PRINCIPLES

A principle is defined as a basic or fundamental truth, law, or assumption on which other truths may depend. In the past, decisions regarding what were the most important things to teach children and what was the best way to teach them were based on principles derived from experience. Though we still depend upon experience in making such decisions today, the current trend is to rely more upon scientific research. The suggestions that follow are supported by both experience and research.

- Learning is proportional to the motivation of the child. Select tasks that afford the greatest opportunity to succeed: success is an important motivational factor.
- Any jackass can kick down a stable door, but it takes a good carpenter to build one: create a good teaching/learning situation. Remove all hazards and unnecessary distractions from the play area. Structure the environment so that the average child can turn in a superior performance.
- Use a positive approach in improving behavior or performance. Avoid belittling children.
- Make every child a winner. Develop the ability to identify and decrease the difficulties children have in learning new skills. Careful placement of children in an activity may enhance their chance for success.
- Keep the learning process challenging, but not overwhelming: break complicated movement patterns down into simple, sequential steps. Teach skills that lead to new skills. When skilled individuals look good while performing, it is because they are in good physical condition and have mastered the sequence of events essential to executing a specific routine.
- When introducing a new activity, discuss briefly but enthusiastically its purpose and importance.
- Children learn motor activities more by imitation than by verbal instruction: demonstrate the activity or select a skillful child to do so, then let *everyone* try it. Always strive for 100 percent participation.
- The rate of learning and the rate of improvement vary from child to child, and readiness 9

1

may be determined by maturation. Give recognition for trying and for improving, as well as for succeeding.

- Help children discover ways to measure their own achievement.
- Provide opportunities for leadership and fellowship as a member of a group or team. Teach children to value other members of their class, social group, and community at large.
- Promote sociability as well as success in team performance, but help children understand the causes of their failures. Teach them never to be satisfied with second place or with losing if they are capable of capturing first or winning.
- Help children to find themselves, to view their lives as a set of unified experiences. Aid them in appreciating their strengths and in overcoming their weaknesses.
- Encourage children to practice to improve their performance. Remember that an individual rarely reaches the limits of his capacity to improve; however, those in poor physical condition rarely improve quickly.

OBJECTIVES

Objectives are the standards or goals to be sought through movement education or activity experiences. Because each child is stuck with the body he has, he should be taught how it works, how it may be developed, and how it may best be maintained. The more he comprehends, the more likely it is that he will do what is necessary for its healthful maintenance.

The primary objective of any activity or movement education program is to further the participants' development in each of these six areas:

1. Physical Fitness. All children should be taught the dimensions and importance of physical fitness. In reality, it implies having the ability to function at one's very best. One cannot be

expected to play any activity well if he lacks the fitness necessary to perform essential movements.

Part of total fitness, physical fitness is a personal attribute influenced by a number of individual factors, including heredity and environment. It is transitory and will disappear unless it is maintained through vigorous exercise.

The major components of fitness are:

- Strength—force a muscle can exert
- Coordination—use of the senses
- Flexibility—maximum range of joint movements
- Stamina—ability to perform repetitive movements
- Speed—ability to move quickly
- Equilibrium—balance
- Power—ability to transfer energy
- Cardiovascular recovery—speed with which the heartbeat returns to normal after exercise is stopped

The physically fit child resists fatigue and disease and has enough resilience to recover quickly from illness or to cope adequately with stress.

2. Motor Skills. Motor skills are reflected in one's muscular coordination and ability during activity performance, and are used in walking, speaking, writing, playing, and manipulating various kinds of objects. Comprehension of perceptual-motor learning, balance, flexibility, general coordination, and mobility is prerequisite to understanding how motor skills are acquired.

3. Health Skills. Nothing is more important than good health. Maximum attention should be given to health concepts, practices, and attitudes with emphasis on safety, posture, relaxation, nutrition, cleanliness, and exercise.

4. Social Skills. Helping children attain social status and make acceptable social adjustments should be a major objective of any program in which children interrelate.

5. Emotional Skills. A large number of cognitive and affective elements intermingle in the development of emotional skills. These elements are judged on a continuum from acceptable to unacceptable. Basic and secondary needs play an extremely important role in emotional development, as do affectional attachments, pleasures, and displeasures.

6. Cognitive Skills. The cognitive skills are the means by which all knowledge is acquired. Together, they constitute the ability to make use of intellectual processes in furthering one's knowledge. They are the faculty of knowing something as distinguished from not knowing it and include, but are more than, intellectual curiosity and problem solving.

BASIC MOVEMENTS

We have good intentions but often demonstrate poor judgment in teaching fundamental movement patterns. Many new patterns are built of existing ones, and their successful performance requires merely transferring old habits to new situations; however, some patterns incorporate new skills. Children find it difficult to acquire new patterns that are based upon skills they have not mastered. For this reason, it is important that basic (part-routine) movements be taught and practiced before full routines are attempted.

Fundamentals are subroutines from which full routines are developed. They include

- the correct way to walk, run, jump, leap, skip, slide, hop, and gallop;
- the correct way to throw, catch, kick, and bounce various kinds of balls;
- good body mechanics, including posture;
- twisting, turning, falling, tumbling, and balance movements;
- a large variety of rhythmic movements;
- manipulative (hula hoop, parachute, beanbag) activities;
- a variety of health and safety procedures; and
- strategy and tactical play.

The activities described and illustrated in the chapters that follow offer many ways for children to master these fundamentals through supervised play. The evaluation forms that are included will provide you with a way to measure their accomplishment.

UPSIDE-DOWN AND INSIDE-OUT

Movement education has developed through an upside-down and inside-out process. We permit children to move in any way they choose. When they appear to have a natural aptitude or talent for good movements, we select them for a team and teach them the fundamental movements a particular sport requires. By this time, many of them have learned inefficient movements that are difficult to correct.

It would seem more logical to teach all children the correct movements in the beginning. Movement education should be viewed as being fundamental to health and happiness, not simply as a fad or a way to blow off steam. It should be based on sound principles developed through experience and research and should be directed toward achieving particular objectives in body development and skill mastery through both knowledge and practice.

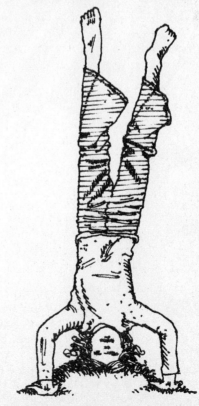

CREATIVE MOVEMENT

3.

Creative movement is an important part of activity programs for children because it does not involve competition. Instead, it offers each child an opportunity to explore, experiment, and develop his own ways of using his body to solve movement problems, and it makes him feel that *any* response he gives to a problem is an acceptable one—so long as he does respond.

Your primary goal in leading creative movement activities should be maximum participation. Because all responses are acceptable and much of the equipment is novel, children do not feel intimidated and are usually eager to take part.

This chapter covers basic movement, manipulative activities, and creative and imaginative activities. The equipment needed for these lessons includes:

- balls (1 for each child)
- beanbags (2 for each child)
- hoops (1 for each child)
- jump ropes (1 for each child)
- parachute (round)
- record player and records
- rhythm instruments (assorted drums, cymbals, sticks, tambourine)
- scoops (can be made from plastic bleach or water containers)
- tennis-type or foam balls (1 for each child)
- wands

Before beginning a creative movement activity,
- establish start and stop signals. You may wish to use a whistle or horn, turn the lights off, or clap your hands.
- demonstrate the correct methods for handling and using any unusual or unfamiliar pieces of equipment, such as the parachute.
- pose problems that can be solved by the children with the physical skills they have.
- emphasize that *any* response is acceptable, but encourage originality and imagination where appropriate.
- make children aware of the presence and proximity of others and of how to avoid collisions or other accidents.

The activities in this chapter progress from simple to complex. Beginning lessons pose one- or two-phase problems, while later lessons pose problems of increased length and difficulty. While you may choose and use them singly or in any order, most groups should begin with the first lesson and do the succeeding lessons in order. To determine where to begin teaching new skills, try parts of several different lessons.

3

BALANCING ACTIVITIES　　　20-30 MIN.

Purpose: Basic movement; balancing skills development
Equipment: Balance beam, 1 beanbag per child, 1 wand per child
Play Area: Playground, gym

Directions:

One at a time on the balance
beam,
- walk forward, then backward.
- balance a beanbag on your head
  (arm, hand) and walk forward
  (backward).

Well spaced on the floor or
ground,
- balance on two (four) parts of
  your body.
- balance on your knees.
- balance a beanbag on your head
  (arm, foot, hand).
- walk (run) a set distance with a
  beanbag on your head.
- balance a wand on different
  parts of your body.

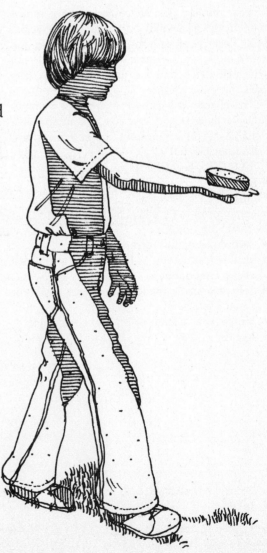

3

WALKING ACTIVITIES   5-10 MIN

Purpose: Basic movement; creative activities
Equipment: Records and record player, rhythm band
Play Area: Gym, classroom, playground

Directions:

In a well-spaced circle or line, walk
- forward along a crack or line painted or taped on the floor or ground.
- backward along the line.
- with short (medium, long) steps.
- following the leader.
- quickly (slowly).
- with your left (right) foot always forward.
- to music, clapping, singing, or the beat of drums or other rhythm instruments.
- ten steps forward and five steps backward until you reach (destination).

Note:

In doing the last activity, vary the number of steps in each direction and the destination.

Related Activities:

Talk about posture: What is posture? Why is good posture important? How are good posture and good health related? For additional ideas, see the section on posture in Chapter 9.

3

15

MAKING A STRAW HORN

Equipment: 1 plastic drinking straw for each child; several pairs of scissors

Directions:
- Flatten about 1 to 2 inches of the straw at one end.
- Use scissors to trim the flattened end to a V.
- Put the V-shaped end in your mouth just behind your lips and blow *hard*.
- Use this musical instrument as you walk and/or clap to music.

Note:
Different lengths of straw will produce different tones: the shorter the straw, the higher the sound.

RUNNING ACTIVITIES   20 MIN.

Purpose: Basic movement
Equipment: None
Play Area: Playground, gym

Directions:
In a well-spaced formation, run
- forward along a crack, line, or shape painted or taped on the floor or ground.
- backward along the line or shape.
- with long (medium, short) steps.
- very quickly (slowly).
- to clapping.
- on your heels to (destination).
- on your tiptoes to (destination).
- ten steps forward, then five backward.

Note:
- In doing the last activity, vary the number of steps in each direction and the destination.
- Allow a rest time between activities.

Related Activities:
Talk about lines and cracks: What is a line? What is a crack? What makes a crack in the sidewalk? What are *expansion, contraction,* and *weathering*?

HOPPING ACTIVITIES   20 MIN.

Purpose: Basic movement; imaginative skills development
Equipment: Record player, records, drum, jump ropes
Play Area: Playground, gym

Directions:
In a well-spaced formation, hop
- in place.
- 10 (15, 20, 25) times on one foot, then the same number of hops on the other foot.
- in place, turning right (left) on one foot, then on the other foot.
- to music or to drumbeats.
- like a rabbit, kangaroo, bird, elephant, frog.
- while jumping rope.

Note:
Hopping is on *one* foot.

3

SKIPPING ACTIVITIES   20 MIN.

Purpose: Basic movement
Equipment: Drum
Play Area: Playground, gym

Directions:
In a well-spaced formation, skip
- to clapping, to drumbeats.
- freely in a designated area (no bumping).
- *in* a line *on* a line (no passing).
- backward on the line.
- forward until the whistle is blown, then backward then forward, etc.
- slowly (quickly).
- with knees high (low).
- with a partner.

Note:
If some of the children have not skipped before or have not skipped for a while, have them practice skipping by stepping forward on the right foot and hopping on the right foot, then stepping foward on the left foot, and hopping on the left foot: step-hop, step-hop.

3

STRETCHING ACTIVITIES 15-20 MIN.

Purpose: Basic movement
Equipment: Bar from which to hang
Play Area: Playground, gym

Directions:
- Standing (sitting, lying down), stretch your whole body.
- Stretch your fingers (hands, neck, feet, legs, arms, chest).
- Stretch yourself out *wide*.
- Reach for spots on the wall (real or imaginary).
- Hang and stretch on some type of bar.
- Jump and stretch.
- Bend one leg and stretch the other (reverse).

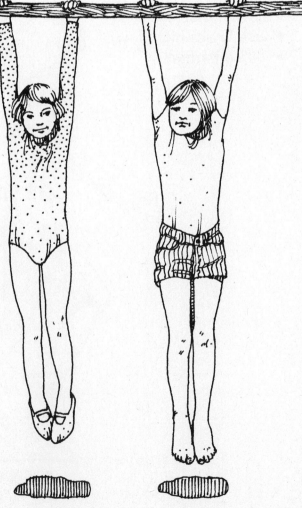

3

TWISTING ACTIVITIES

15-20 MIN.

Purpose: Basic movement
Equipment: None
Play Area: Gym, playground

Directions:

- While sitting (standing, lying down, kneeling), twist as many parts of your body as you can.
- Twist your body to the right (left).
- Twist your body in two (three) different directions at the same time.
- Make your body wide (narrow) and twist it.
- Twist some parts of your body fast and some slow at the same time.

- Standing still, twist one (then both) arms around your body.
- Holding your head still, twist your trunk as far as possible in one direction, then reverse.
- Twist your head and see how much you can see behind you.
- Twist your trunk from right to left while walking.

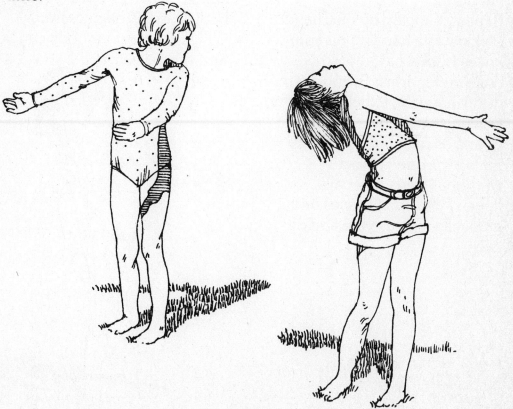

3

21

SWINGING AND TURNING ACTIVITIES

15-20 MIN.

Purpose: Basic movement
Equipment: Bar from which to hang; box, chair, or bench
Play Area: Playground, gym

Directions:

- Swing one arm across your body. Vary the speed of swings. Repeat with your other arm.
- Swing your head from side to side. Swing it forward and backward.
- Lying down, swing one leg back and forth. Repeat with your other leg, then both legs.
- Hang from a bar, holding on with both hands, and swing back and forth.
- Repeat, hanging by one hand.
- Swing while hanging by your knees from a bar.
- Swing your arms. Swing again, using the swing to help you jump as high as possible.
- Rotate as many of your body parts as possible. Start with small parts (eyeballs, fingers) and small circles and gradually increase the size of each.

- Turn while walking, running, hopping, skipping, galloping.
- Turn around a box, chair, bench.
- Hold hands and then turn with a partner.
- Move around a circle (square, the play area, etc.) while turning with a partner.
- Kneel down, put your hands on the ground, and make your hands "walk" around your body, turning as necessary.
- Which part of your body can you turn the fastest?

LIFTING ACTIVITIES   20 MIN.

Purpose: Basic movement; imaginative activities
Equipment: None
Play Area: Gym, playground

Directions:

- While lying down, lift your left (right) arm off the ground and then return it to its original position. Repeat several times.
- Lying down, lift your left (right) leg off the ground and return it to its original position. Lift and lower both legs.
- Standing, lift one arm at a time. Repeat.
- Standing, lift one leg, then the opposite leg. Reverse.
- Lift an imaginary box, rock, baby, apple, car, balloon.
- Lift an imaginary box and put it on a high shelf.

Related Activities:

Talk about muscles. Use the section in Chapter 9 and the poster for ideas. Where are the body's strongest lifting muscles located? (In the thigh.) What stance enables you to use these muscles and protect your back when you must lift a heavy object? (Keeping your back straight, bending your knees, lifting by pushing with and straightening your legs.)

3

HOOP ACTIVITIES

20 MIN.

Purpose: Developing manipulative skills
Equipment: 1 hoop per child, 1 beanbag per child
Play Area: Gym, playground

3

Directions:

- Hold your hoop overhead, then bring it down on your right (left) side. Use a count of 4 for each side. Repeat.
- Hold your hoop on one side of your body. Sit down without letting go of your hoop, then stand again. Repeat.
- Spin your hoop like a top. As it spins, run around it.
- Lay your hoop on the ground. Try to throw your beanbag into the hoop. Aim for its center. Back farther and farther away from the hoop.
- Spin your hoop on your right (left) wrist.
- Hula your hoop around your neck (waist, knees). Try this with more than one hoop.
- Spin your hoop around the ankle of one foot. Jump over it with your other foot as it spins.
- Roll your hoop and run to get it. Jump through it two (three) times as it rolls.

PARACHUTE ACTIVITIES   20-30 MIN.

Purpose: Developing manipulative skills
Equipment: Round parachute
Play Area: Playground, gym
Formation: Well-spaced circle around chute.

Directions:

Before beginning these activities,
- establish start and stop signals ("1, 2, 3, lift").
- demonstrate the correct grip (overhand with one or both hands). Everyone must hold on unless otherwise instructed.
- stretch out the parachute on the ground or floor.
- have children space themselves evenly around the chute.
- have children grasp the chute at the edge and hold it waist high, each one pulling it gently toward him.

To do these activities:
- Grasp the chute and walk to the left. Stop. Walk to the right.
- Grasp the chute and run to the left. Stop. Run to the right.
- Kneeling and continuing to hold on, put the chute on the ground. On the signal ("1, 2, 3, lift"), stand and raise your arms—and the chute—overhead.
- On the count of 3, raise the chute, then bring it down to the floor and kneel on it, making a "mushroom."
- Raise the chute and release it on command ("Let go"). It will float down to the floor.
- On command, raise the chute. Ask two children to change places by running under the raised chute to the opposite side. Gradually increase the number running under until it includes all the children.
- Raise the chute, step inside it, and pull it down over you to the floor as you kneel inside your "cave."
- Hold the chute at waist height, pulling it gently toward you and working your arms up and down vigorously to make waves. Add some rubber or beach balls and watch the "popcorn."

Related Activities:
- What is a parachute made of?
- What is a parachute used for?
- Who invented the parachute? When?
- How does it work?

3

ROPE ACTIVITIES 1   10-20 MIN.

Purpose: Developing manipulative and rhythmic skills
Equipment: 1 rope per child
Play Area: Playground, gym
Formation: Well-spaced circle. Each child holds his rope to his right
(left) side with one hand holding each end of the rope.

Directions:
- Turn the rope in a sideways swing clockwise.
- Continue turning to a count of 1 (down), 2 (up).
- Repeat the same procedure counterclockwise.
- Gradually increase the speed of the rope turns.
- Gradually decrease the speed of the rope turns.
- After some practice, alternate forward and backward patterns.
- Make up your own patterns.

Note:
Watch spacing.

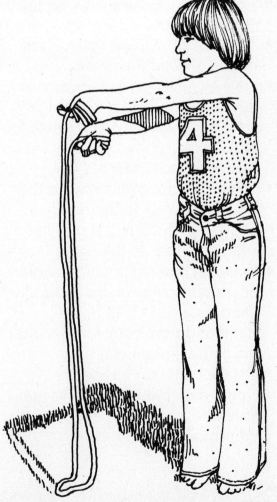

ROPE ACTIVITIES 2   10-20 MIN.

Purpose: Developing manipulative skills
Equipment: 1 rope per child
Play Area: Playground, gym
Formation: Well-spaced circle. Each child holds the ends of his rope together overhead.

Directions:

- Swing the rope clockwise (counterclockwise) in a circle above your head.
- After some practice, swing the rope in a circle to a count of 10. (Each number counted slowly indicates a completed circle with the rope.)
- Reverse for a count of 10.
- Alternate five clockwise and five counterclockwise circles.

- After practicing, combine overhead swinging with that of left- and right-sided swinging.
- Create a pattern using these rope swings.

3

ROPE ACTIVITIES 3   10-20 MIN.

Purpose: Developing manipulative skills
Equipment: 1 rope per child
Play Area: Playground, gym
Formation: Well-spaced circle or free formation. Each child holds one end of his rope in each hand and "turns" it.

Directions:

- Jump your rope, landing on the balls of your feet. Hop a second time as your rope passes overhead ("rebound") from front to back. Repeat many times.
- Repeat this activity, turning your rope "backward" (from front to back).
- Create a pattern using jumps forward and backward.
- Jump over your rope on your left foot; rebound on your left foot. Repeat several times.
- Jump over your rope on your right foot; rebound on your right foot. Repeat.
- Create a pattern using left and right foot jumps and rebounds. Demonstrate your pattern to the group.

3

ROPE ACTIVITIES 4   20-30 MIN.

Purpose: Developing manipulative skills
Equipment: 1 rope per child; music if desired
Record: Educational Activities Album 12
Play Area: Playground, gym
Formation: Well-spaced circle or free formation. Each child holds one end of his rope in each hand.

Directions:

1. Jump Skip (side 7)
- Hold your rope behind your ankles.
- Swing it overhead, and jump over it as it passes under your feet.
- Do this in time to music.
- For variation, swing your rope backward (front to back).

2. Hop Skip
- Stand on one foot and hop over your rope as it comes overhead toward your foot.
- Repeat on your other foot.

3. Leap Skip
- Stand on your left foot and hold your rope behind your ankle.
- Swing your rope overhead and down toward your foot.
- Spring over your rope and land on your right foot. Rebound on your right foot.
- Spring over your rope again and land on your left foot. Rebound on your left foot.
- Repeat

29

ROPE ACTIVITIES 5   20-30 MIN.

Purpose: Developing manipulative skills
Equipment: 1 rope per child
Play Area: Playground, gym
Formation: Well-spaced circle or free formation. Each child holds one
end of his rope in each hand

3

Directions:
Jump as you say
- the alphabet

- Cinderella,
  Dressed in white,
  Went upstairs
  To turn on the lights.
  How many lights
  Did she use?
  1, 2, 3, 4, 5, . . .

- One, two,
  Buckle my shoe.
  Three, four
  Shut the door.
  Five, six,
  Pick up sticks.
  Seven, eight,
  Lay them straight.
  Nine, ten,
  A big fat hen.
  Eleven, twelve,
  Ring the bell.
  Thirteen, fourteen,
  Maids a-courting.
  Fifteen, sixteen,
  Girls a-fixing.
  Seventeen, eighteen,
  Boys a-waiting.
  Nineteen, twenty,
  That's a-plenty.

- *(Name) be nimble,*
  And (name) be quick.
  (Name) jump over
  The candlestick.

  Oh jump and jump
  And jump so high,
  But you'd better jump out
  Or (name of child who is next in
  line) will cry.

Note:
This last rhyme is intended for situations where one long rope is being used, and children must take turns jumping and turning. After the rhyme has been recited, the jumper jumps out, and the person who is next in line jumps in.

BEANBAG ACTIVITIES   20 MIN.

Purpose: Developing manipulative skills
Equipment: 1 beanbag per child
Play Area: Gym or playground

Directions:

While standing well spaced,

- throw your beanbag up and catch it.
- throw and catch with a partner.
- toss your beanbag up and clap your hands one (two, three, four) times before catching it.
- toss your beanbag up, turn around in a circle, and catch it.
- toss your beanbag forward, and run up to catch it.
- balance your beanbag on your head (hand, shoulder, arm). Without letting the beanbag fall, walk around, sit down, and stand again.
- toss your beanbag to yourself from your elbow and from between your feet, your knees.
- pick up your beanbag from the floor or ground with the toes on your left (right) foot and hold it while you hop on your right (left) foot to another spot.
- toss your beanbag toward a designated target (hoop, wastebasket) from a specified distance. Increase the distance.

While sitting well spaced,

- toss your beanbag up and catch it.
- throw and catch with a partner.

RELAXING ACTIVITIES

Purpose: To relax
Equipment: None
Play Area: Playground, gym
Formation: Well-spaced lines, circle, or free formation.

Directions:

1. Hands

- Open and shut your hands. Clench your fists, then open your hands, extending the fingers as far as possible.
- Rotate your right (left) wrist clockwise (counterclockwise).
- Rotate your thumbs clockwise (counterclockwise).

2. Head

- Roll your head in a clockwise (counterclockwise) circle.
- Tip your head forward, backward, right, and left.
- Bounce your head up and down, bringing your chin as close to your chest as possible on each bounce.

3. Shoulders

- Rotate your right (left) shoulder forward (backward).
- Raise your shoulders as high as possible, then return them to their original position.
- Raise your right (left) shoulder, then return it to its original position.

4. Body

- Standing with your feet a shoulders' width apart, bend from the waist and bounce, touching your hands to the floor ten times.
- Lying on your back and starting with your feet, tighten and relax each part of your body (feet, lower legs, upper legs, hands, arms, stomach, back, face).
- How many ways can you move and relax the upper half of your body without moving the lower half?
- How many ways can you move and relax the lower half of your body without moving the upper half?

3

33

RHYTHMS
AND DANCE

4.

This chapter covers recreational folk dances, traditional social dance steps, and skills for square dancing. For children aged eight through twelve, emphasis should be placed on learning set patterns of dance steps and on refining rhythmic movement. The activities included in this chapter have thus been chosen to develop these basic skills; however, they must be repeated several times over a period of weeks to ensure skill development.

Activities in this chapter are arranged to progress from simple to complex. Evaluation forms interspersed among chapter activities should help you decide the level at which to begin.

In teaching rhythmic movement or dance,
- choose a room with adequate acoustics.
- choose music with strong, clear tone and beat.
- walk through the dance to be taught before the instruction session, and listen to the musical accompaniment all the way through.
- give as little instruction as necessary, and allow the children to participate as much as possible.

ELEMENTS OF RHYTHM

Tempo—The speed of the music or beat.

Beat—The underlying rhythmic quality of the music, either even or uneven.

Meter—The organization and combination of beats to form a measure.

Measure—The defined number of beats dividing the composition evenly into parts.

Time Signature—Indicates the number of beats found in a measure, and what note receives one beat.

Example: $\quad 2 =$ beats per measure
$\quad\quad\quad \overline{4} =$ quarter note receives one beat

Accents—The notes or beats that are emphasized.

Intensity—The force of the accompaniment (loud, soft, heavy, light).

Phrase—The pattern or grouping of measures. Commonly, phrases are groupings of 8 or 16 measures.

Pattern—The arrangement of phrases into chorus and verse.

4

TERMS

Allemande left—Join hands with corner, left to left, and walk all the way around to place.

Banjo position—Social dance position, right hip to right hip.

Balance—Step toward partner with one foot (both use same foot), touch toe of other foot alongside. Reverse to step back to original position.

Bleking step—Spring into air onto one foot, extend other foot to front, toe up. Hop again and switch position of feet.

Corner—Person (not partner) to left of boy and right of girl in a square.

Do-si-do—Facing each other, partners walk toward each other, pass right shoulders, pass back-to-back, pass left shoulders and then back up to original position.

Face-to-face, back-to-back step—Partners facing, boy holds girl's left hand in his right. Together, they take two steps sideways, swinging their arms forward to end back-to-back. Then repeat, swinging their arms backward to end facing each other.

Grand right and left—Facing each other, partners join right hands, walk past each other, and extend left hands to next person in the circle or square. They continue around the circle or square until told to stop or until partners meet again.

Grapevine—Step to side, step behind, step to side, step in front.

Home—Original or starting position.

Longways set—Five or six couples standing in two straight lines facing each other with boys on one side and girls on the other.

Polka—Hop, step, close, step; uneven rhythm.

Promenade—Partners join hands in skaters' position and walk to home position.

Inside foot—In single formation, the foot closest to circle center when facing clockwise or counterclockwise; for couples, the foot closest to partner when both are facing clockwise or counterclockwise.

Outside foot—In single formation, the foot farthest away from circle center when facing clockwise or counterclockwise; for couples, the foot farthest away from partner when standing side by side facing clockwise or counterclockwise.

Mazurka step—Hop on one foot, brushing the other foot across shin at same time. Step forward with raised leg, close.

Schottische step—Walk forward left, right, left, and hop on left foot; walk forward right, left, right, and hop on right foot.

Sidecar position—Social dance position, left hip to left hip.

Step close—Step forward or sideways with one foot. Close/draw the other alongside.

Toe-heel step—Hop on the right foot, extending the left foot to the side with the toe pointed. Hop again on the right foot and point the left toe up, heel to ground. Repeat, hopping on the left foot.

Two-step—Step, close, step, touch.

Waltz
   Progressive—Three walking steps in the line of direction, accenting the first step.
   Box—Forward, side, together; back, side, together.

4

BASIC FORMATIONS

Double circle with partners facing; boys standing with backs to circle center.

Single circle facing either center, clockwise (pictured), or counterclockwise.

Double circle with partners facing either clockwise (pictured) or counterclockwise, or with sets of partners facing.

Single circle with partners facing one another.

4

POSITIONS

Inside hands held.

Arms around waists.

Skaters' position: partners stand side by side, extend inside arms to hold left to left hand, right to right hand.

4

Two hands held.

Shoulder-waist position: boy's hands on girl's waist; girl's hands on boy's shoulders.

Social dance position: boy's right hand on girl's waist, left hand extended; girl's left hand on boy's shoulder, right hand extended.

Varsouvienne position: boy stands slightly behind girl and extends arms to sides; girl extends arms to join boy's hands.

DANCES

Dance Description Chart

Name of Dance	Country of Origin	Difficulty	Basic Steps	Page
Hora	Israel	Easy	Step-hop	42
All-American Promenade	USA	Easy	Walk, balance	43
Double Clap Polka	Czechoslovakia	Easy	Progressive polka	44
Kentwood Schottische	USA	Easy	Schottische, step-hop	45
Patty-cake Polka	USA	Easy	Heel-toe, slide	46
Virginia Reel	USA	Easy	Walking, skipping, reel	47
Alunelul	Rumania	Moderate	Stamp, side step	50
Put Your Little Foot	USA	Moderate	Mazurka step	51
Lili Marlene	USA	Moderate	Polka, slide	53
Oxdansen	Sweden	Moderate	Stamp, spring	54
Lummi Stick Dance	South Pacific Islands	Moderate	Hand movements	56
Teton Mountain Stomp	USA	Moderate	Walking, social dance position variations	58
Scottish Sword Dance	Scotland	Advanced	Schottische	59
Gathering Peasecods	England	Advanced	Walk, slide, individual turn in place	62
The Two-Step	USA	Advanced	Two-step	64
Tea for Two	USA	Advanced	Two-step	66
Rye Waltz	USA	Advanced	Waltz	69
Hot Time	USA	Advanced	Square dance	70
Grand Square	USA	Advanced	Square dance	72
Tinikling	Philippines	Advanced	Hop	74
Old Dobbin	USA	Advanced	Shuffle walk	76

4

HORA   ISRAEL

Basic Steps: Step-hop, side step   2/4 time
Records: Folkraft F1106B, 1116A; RCA LPM 1623
Formation: Closed circle, single formation. Hands on shoulders of
                 people on both sides.

Steps	*Measures*
Step to left side with left foot. Step right behind left.	**1**
Step to left side with left foot, hop on left, swing right across left.	**2**
Step on right in place, hop on right, swing left across right.	**3**

Repeat measures 1-3 to end of record.

Related Activities:
- Where is Israel?
- Why and when was it established?
- What countries surround it?
- What is the terrain like? The weather?

ALL-AMERICAN PROMENADE   USA

Basic Steps: Walk, balance   4/4 time
Records: Windsor A754, 7605
Formation: Double circle, boys on inside, couples facing
counterclockwise with inside hands joined.

Steps	*Measures*
Boys on left foot, girls on right, walk forward 4 steps. On the fourth step, pivot on the inside foot, turning one-half turn toward partner to end with back facing line of direction.	**1-4**
Back up 4 steps in line of direction. Pivot toward partner one-half turn on fourth step to end in original position.	**5-8**
Balance together, balance apart (step together with inside feet, touch outside foot alongside, reverse).	**9-10**
Boy steps 3 times in place. Girl crosses in front of boy in 3 steps to change sides.	**11-12**
Repeat measures 11-12.	**13-14**
Boy moves forward in 4 walking steps to new partner. Girl twirls in place in 4 steps, turning to her right.	**15-16**

Repeat entire dance to end of record.

Related Activities:

- Did a pioneer boy or girl have more or less leisure time than you have? Discuss.
- Without movies, television, and professional sports, what did the pioneers do for fun?

- Talk about the importance of dances to the pioneers as a means of entertainment and a form of social interplay.

DOUBLE CLAP POLKA   CZECHOSLOVAKIA

Basic Step: Polka   2/4 time
Records: Folkraft F1413, Folk Dancer MH-3016, Educational Dance
               Recordings FD-2
Formation: Double circle facing counterclockwise; varsouvienne
               position, boys on inside of circle.
Polka Step: Hop on left, forward right, close left, forward right. Hop on
               right, forward left, close right, forward left.

Steps	*Measures*
Starting with weight on left foot, take 16 polka steps counterclockwise, leaning to the side of the lead foot and expanding the circle.	**1-16**
Change hand positions: Girl places left hand on boy's right shoulder, right hand on her hip. Boy places his right hand over girl's right hand and extends his left arm forward at shoulder height. Walk forward 32 steps. As couples walk forward, circle "shrinks" until each boy is able to place his left hand on the left shoulder of the boy in front of him.	**17-32**
Boys stop, face center of circle, clap own hands together twice, and turn palms out to slap hands of people on both sides once. Repeat this sequence 16 times. Moving counterclockwise, girls do 16 polka steps around boys.	**33-48**

Take new partners and start the dance from the beginning. Tell anyone who is without a partner to move to the center of circle, find a partner, and rejoin the others.

Note:
Each time the dance is repeated, expand the circle during the first 16 measures.

KENTWOOD SCHOTTISCHE   USA

Basic Steps: Schottische   4/4 time
Record: Any good schottische music
Formation: Double circle facing counterclockwise; boys on inside,
                         inside hands joined.
Schottische Step: Walk forward right, left, right, hop in place on right.
                                 Walk forward left, right, left, hop in place on left.

Steps	*Measures*
With boys starting on the left foot and girls on the right, take 4 schottische steps forward.	**1-4**
Move away from partner in 1 schottische step, clapping own hands together on the hop. Partners move together in 1 schottische step, slapping both partner's hands on the hop.	**5-6**
Hook right elbows and turn 1 circle in place with 4 step-hops.	**7-8**
Repeat measures 5-8, hooking left elbows for the step-hop turn.	**9-12**
Resume original position, moving counterclockwise. Boy moves forward 4 schottische steps. Girl moves forward 2 schottische steps, then does 2 schottische steps in place to take a new partner.	**13-16**

Repeat from the beginning.

Related Activity:
A schottische step is a Scottish dance step. Talk about Scotland. Where is it? For what textile design pattern and what fabric is it best known? (Plaid, wool.) What is a *tartan*?

PATTY-CAKE POLKA   USA

Basic Steps: Heel-toe step, slide   2/4 time
Records: Folkraft F1177A, 1260; RCA 1625
Formation: Double circle, partners facing, both hands clasped; boys'
              backs to circle center.
Heel-Toe Step: Hop on left foot, right foot to side, point toe up, heel on
              floor. Hop on left foot again, point right toe to side of
              left foot. Repeat, hopping on right foot.

Steps	Measures
With boy's weight on left foot and girl's weight on right foot, take 2 heel-toe steps.	**1-2**
Slide counterclockwise 4 steps.	**3-4**
Repeat measures 1-4 using opposite feet and sliding clockwise.	**5-8**
Clap partner's right hand with own right hand; clap own hands together.	**9**
Clap partner's left hand with own left hand; clap own hands together.	**10**
Clap both partner's hands; clap own hands together.	**11**
Slap own knees; clap own hands together.	**12**
Hook right elbows and skip 4 steps in a small circle.	**13-14**
Partners split. Each moves left to new partner in 4 walking steps.	**15-16**
Repeat dance from beginning.	

4

Related Activities:
Discuss the features of your body's construction that make dancing possible. What if we had bones, but no joints? Could bones move without muscles? What attaches bones to bones at the joints? (Ligaments.) What attaches muscles to bones? (Tendons.) How does your brain tell your muscles to move? For additional related material, see Chapter 9.

VIRGINIA REEL   USA

Basic Steps: Walk, skip, reel   4/4 or 2/4 time
Records: MacGregor 735A; RCA LPM 1623; or any good square
          dance music
Formation: Longways sets of 4 or 5 couples, partners facing. Designate
          one end of set as "head," other as "foot."
Do-si-do: Walk forward, pass right shoulder to right shoulder,
          back-to-back, left shoulder to left shoulder, then return to
          original position, backing into place.

Steps	*Measures*
1. With boys starting on the left foot and girls on the right, all walk forward 3 steps, bow/curtsy, and walk backward 4 steps to place.	**1-8**
2. Repeat.	
3. All walk forward, do-si-do, passing right shoulders first, and return to starting position in 8 walking steps.	**1-8**
4. Repeat, passing left shoulders first, then back-to-back, right shoulders, and back up to original ("home") position.	
5. Reel: Head "gent," foot "lady" skip to center, hook right elbows, turn around once, and return to home position (8 skips).	**1-8**
6. Head lady and foot gent do the same.	
7. Repeat preceding 8 measures, hooking left elbows.	**1-8**
8. Head lady and gent hook right elbows and skip 4 steps in a circle. Break and hook left elbows with next person in line (head gent goes to lady, head lady goes to gent). Return to partner and circle once. Return to next in line. Head couple repeats this step, moving down the middle of the set, until	**1-32**

all in line have had a turn and head couple reaches the foot of the line. Head couple skips to home position.

9. Head lady and gent join hands and slide 4 steps to foot of line, then slide 4 steps in opposite direction.   **1-8**

10. Head lady and gent turn to outside and skip to foot of line; all others follow. Head lady and gent face each other, clasp hands, and raise their arms to form an arch. Others pass under the arch. Reform the set with a new head couple and old head couple now at the foot.   **1-32**

11. Repeat entire dance until all couples have had a chance to be head couple.

Note:
Tell children to clap their hands to the music when they are not dancing.

Related Activity:
Review new terms and their meanings:
- Longways set
- Do-si-do
- Lady
- Gent
- Head
- Foot
- Head couple
- Home or home position

EVALUATION

Area: Rhythms and Dance

Name _____ **Date of Observation** _____

Dance	Check one or more
1. Hora	Moves in time to music ☐ Does not move in time to music ☐ Changes direction of movement smoothly ☐
2. Double Clap Polka	Can do progressive polka step ☐ Cannot do progressive polka step ☐
3. Kentwood Schottische	Can do progressive schottische step ☐ Cannot do progressive schottische step ☐
4. Virginia Reel	Can move and clap in time to music ☐ Cannot move and clap in time to music ☐ Remembers routine ☐ Does not remember routine ☐

4

ALUNELUL   RUMANIA

Basic Steps: Stamp, side step   2/4 time
Records: Folk Dancer MH 1120; Elektra 1120
Formation: Single circle, all facing circle center and clasping forearms of
dancers on either side.

Steps	*Measures*
Moving to the right, step on right foot, then step on left foot behind right. Step on right, left behind, step on right. Stamp left heel twice. (5 steps)	**1-4**
Moving to left, step on left foot, right behind, step on left, right behind, step on left. Stamp right heel twice.	**5-8**
Moving to right, step on right foot, left behind, step on right. Stamp left heel once. (3 steps)	**9-10**
Moving to left, step on left foot, right behind, step on left. Stamp right heel once.	**11-12**
In place, step on right foot, stamp left heel. Step on left foot, stamp right heel.	**13-14**
Repeat measures 13-14.	**15-16**
Repeat dance from the beginning.	

Related Activities:
The dance title means "little hazelnut." What does a hazelnut look like? Is a hazelnut edible? What other kinds of nuts are edible? Is a peanut really a nut? To what plant family does the peanut belong?

PUT YOUR LITTLE FOOT   USA

Basic Step: Mazurka step   3/4 time
Records: Folkraft 1165, World of Fun 107B, Folk Dancer MH-3016,
        Windsor 7615B
Formation: Double circle facing counterclockwise; boys on inside,
        couples in varsouvienne position.
Mazurka Step: Start with weight on left foot. Hop on left foot, sweeping
        right foot across left shin. Step forward on right, close
        left, and extend right foot slightly forward to begin
        sweep motion again.

Steps		*Measures*
Part I	Boys and girls begin on the left foot and take 2 mazurka steps forward.	**1-2**
	With weight on the left foot, hop on left foot, sweep right across left. Walk right, left, right, and point left foot forward.	**3-4**
	Repeat measures 1-4, starting on the opposite (right) foot.	**5-8**
	Repeat measures 1-2.	**9-10**
	With weight on the left foot, hop on the left foot, and sweep the right foot across the left shin. Walk right, left. Holding hands, both pivot to left as they step forward on right and point left in new line of direction (clockwise).	**11-12**
	Repeat measures 9-12, beginning on the opposite (right) foot. Pivot will cause couples to face counterclockwise once again.	**13-16**
Part II	Walk to right (45-degree angle), right, left, right. Point left foot to front and hold.	**1-2**
	Walk to left (45-degree angle), left, right, left. Point right foot to front and hold.	**3-4**
	Repeat measures 1-2.	**5-6**

Drop hands. Boy advances to next partner in 4 steps. Girl twirls in place clockwise in 4 steps.

7-8

Begin dance again with new partner.

Related Activities:
This dance was popular during colonial days, and is an American version of a French dance called the Varsouvienne. What customs did the colonists bring to this country from their European homelands?

4

LILI MARLENE

USA

Basic Steps: Polka, slides

2/4 time

Records: World of Fun M-113A; E-Z 78, 6011A

Formation: Double circle, partners facing counterclockwise with inside hands joined.

Face-to-Face, Back-to-Back Step: Partners face each other; boy holds girl's left hand in his right. Boy starts with his weight on his right foot; girl, with her weight on her left. Together they move counterclockwise (sideways) 1 polka step. They swing their arms forward and pivot on the last step of the polka to end back-to-back. They move counterclockwise 1 polka step on the opposite foot, swinging their arms backward at the end so that they face each other once again.

Steps	*Measures*
Walk forward 4 steps.	**1-2**
Face partner. Slide 4 steps counterclockwise with boy starting on left foot and girl on right.	**3-4**
Repeat measures 1-4, moving clockwise with boy starting on right foot and girl starting on left.	**5-8**
Face partner. With boy starting on left foot and girl on right, step in place and hop-swing other leg across. Repeat step, hop, and swing on opposite foot.	**9-10**
Both roll counterclockwise 3 steps, turning away from partner. Hold last count with touch.	**11-12**
Repeat measures 9-12, beginning on opposite foot.	**13-16**
Do face-to-face, back-to-back step 4 times in counterclockwise direction.	**17-24**
Repeat dance from the beginning.	

OXDANSEN

SWEDEN

Basic Steps: Stamp, spring

2/4 time

Record: Folk Dancer MH 1055B

Formation: Couples facing, well spaced, scattered around room.

Steps		Measures
Chorus	With hands on hips, stamp twice, then spring alternately from foot to foot. Boy stamps left foot, springs left, right, left. Girl stamps right foot, springs right, left, right.	**1-2**
Part I	Boy bows, girl curtsies.	**1-2**
	Reverse: boy curtsies, girl bows.	**3-4**
	Repeat measures 1-4.	**5-8**
	Repeat measures 1-8, double time.	**9-16**
Chorus	Repeat measures 1-2 (Chorus).	
Part II	Both extending right foot forward first, partners do bleking steps (hop on one foot, extend other foot forward, toe up; hop and reverse position of feet).	**1-2**
	Repeat measures 1-2 (Part II), hopping in place and extending left foot forward first.	**3-4**
	Repeat measures 1-4 (Part II).	**5-8**
	Repeat measures 1-8 (Part II), double time.	**9-16**
Chorus	Repeat measures 1-2 (Chorus).	
Part III	Partners place own hands on hips with elbows extended to sides and spread feet slightly. Both twist to right to "strike" right elbows, twist to left to strike left elbows.	**1-2**
	Repeat measures 1-2 (Part III).	**3-8**
	Repeat measures 1-8 (Part III), double time.	**9-16**

54

Chorus   Repeat measures 1-2 (Chorus).

Part IV   Partners make faces at each other, each trying   **1-8**
to make the other smile.

Repeat measures 1-8 (Part IV), double time.   **9-16**

Chorus   Repeat measures 1-2 (Chorus).

Part V   Repeat Part I.   **1-16**

Chorus   Repeat measures 1-2 (Chorus).

Note:

In Sweden, male freshmen
entering college are called "oxen."
As a type of hazing,
upperclassmen make oxen
perform this dance as a mock
battle. If at any time during the
dance the oxen smile, they must
begin the dance again.

4

LUMMI STICK DANCE

SOUTH PACIFIC ISLANDS

Record: Koo-EE (Lummi Stick), Twinson Company   3/4 time

Equipment: 1 pair of 8-inch long dowell "sticks" 1 inch in diameter for each child

Formation: Sets of 4 dancers kneeling in a square, with partners facing. Partners should be 2 to 3 feet apart. All 4 dancers in each square perform at the same time. The dance is divided into six parts, and for each part there are two groups of steps, one designated A and the other designated B. One pair of partners within each set should do A, while the other pair does B.

Steps		*Measures*
Chorus	Strike sticks vertically (ends) on the ground, cross own sticks, and strike twice in crossing motion.	**1**
	Repeat measure 1 (floor, cross, cross) 7 times.	**2-8**
Part I		
A	Strike floor, cross, cross. Strike floor, cross, reach forward with right hand and strike partner's right stick.	**1-8**
B	Strike floor, cross, reach forward with right hand, strike partner's right stick. Strike floor, cross, cross.	**1-8**
Chorus	Repeat measures 1-8 (Chorus).	
Part II		
A	Strike floor, cross, cross. Strike floor, reach across, strike right sticks, strike left sticks.	**1-8**
B	Strike floor, reach across, strike right sticks, strike left sticks. Strike floor, cross, cross.	**1-8**

4

Chorus Part III	Repeat measures 1-8 (Chorus).	
A	Strike floor, cross, cross. Strike floor, toss right stick to partner. This "pass" step should be done so that the sticks remain vertical (do not tumble end over end).	**1-8**
B	Strike floor, toss-pass right stick to partner. Strike floor, cross, cross. (*Variation:* Flip one stick in own hand.)	**1-8**
Chorus	Repeat measures 1-8 (Chorus).	
Part IV	Repeat Part III, adding double toss-pass using right and left sticks. (*Variation:* Flip both sticks in own hands.)	**1-8**
Chorus Part V	Repeat measures 1-8 (Chorus).	
A and B	Strike floor, cross, cross. Strike floor, lay right-hand stick on ground and roll to person on the right. At same time, switch left-hand stick to right hand for easy pick up.	**1-8**
Chorus Part VI	Repeat measures 1-8 (Chorus).	
A and B	Repeat Part V, passing left stick in roll.	
Chorus	Repeat measures 1-8 (Chorus).	

Note:

Let children create their own
movements to add to the dance.

TETON MOUNTAIN STOMP   USA

Basic Steps: Walk in social dance, banjo, sidecar positions   4/4 time
Records: Windsor A 753, 7615; Western Jubilee 725
Formation: Single circle, partners facing (boy facing counterclockwise, girl facing clockwise), social dance position.

Directions have been written for boy; girl uses opposite foot.

Steps	*Measures*
Moving toward circle center, step left, close right, step left, stamp right.	**1-2**
Moving away from circle center, step right, close left, step right, stamp left.	**3-4**
Step left, stamp right; step right, stamp left.	**5-6**
Starting with the left foot, walk forward 4 steps.	**7-8**
Shift to banjo position and walk forward 4 more steps. Pivot halfway around to sidecar position. Walk backward 4 steps.	**9-12**
Pivot back to banjo position (facing counterclockwise). Walk 4 steps.	**13-14**
Stop. Boy twirls girl under his left arm and she moves forward to next partner.	**15-16**

Begin dance from measure 1.

Related Activities:
● Where are the Teton Mountains?
● What other major mountain ranges are found in the United States?

SCOTTISH SWORD DANCE   SCOTLAND

Basic Step: Schottische   4/4 time
Record: Any good schottische music, or dance can be performed to
          drumbeat or to tempo of schottische step as set by leader
Formation: Groups of 8 lined up single file. Each dancer carries a
          yardstick or other stick to use as a "sword." Glue cross
          pieces on each stick about 4 inches from one end to
          resemble hand shield.

Steps	*Measures*
Each dancer holds his sword in his right hand, resting the "tip" on his right shoulder. Starting on the right foot, all dancers follow the leader as she winds the line into a circle moving counterclockwise.	**1-16**
Dancers continue doing schottische step, pivot in place, turning toward circle center, and do schottische step moving clockwise.	**16-24**
Dancers continue doing schottische step. Each dancer lowers his sword slowly toward the outside (left) hand of the dancer in front of him. Each dancer looks to left as he moves, then grasps lowered sword of dancer behind in his free left hand. All dancers are now linked by swords.	**24-32**
Dancers stop moving forward but continue doing schottische step in place without breaking their left-hand hold on the sword of the dancer behind. Starting with lead dancer, each dancer takes 2 schottische step counts to step over his sword (held in his right hand), raising his left hand overhead as he pivots halfway around to end facing clockwise.	**32-48**
Moving clockwise, dancers take schottische steps forward.	**48-52**
Dancers stop moving forward but continue doing schottische step in place. Individually they pivot to the left one quarter turn, raising right hand overhead. All end facing circle center with sword held in right hand on top of sword held in left.	**52-56**

59

Continuing to do the schottische step in place, each dancer slides his hands apart, crossing the swords he holds until his hands touch those of the dancers on either side of him. Each dancer, focusing his attention on the sword in his left hand, "hooks" the tip of that sword over the tip of the sword held by the dancer on his left side. Swords should form a "shield."   **56-64**

When the shield is secure, the lead dancer lifts it overhead, and the other dancers follow his serpentine schottische movement until the music ends.   **64-80**

Note:
All dancers must work slowly and in unison to form the shield.

Related Activities:
This dance was performed prior to battle by families/clans of Scotchmen. It was believed that, if the shield formed would hold until the bagpipes ended their tune, all would return from battle safely.
- What other superstitions influenced men in the past?
- What superstitions influence people today?
- How do people come to be superstitious?
- How can superstitions affect their lives? Our lives?

4

EVALUATION

Area: Rhythms and Dance

Name _____ **Date of Observation** _____

Dance	Check one or more	
1. Alunelul	Changes directions with ease	☐
	Changes directions awkwardly	☐
2. Put Your Little Foot	Can perform mazurka step	☐
	Cannot perform mazurka step	☐
3. Lili Marlene	Can perform polka step	☐
	Cannot perform polka step	☐
4. Lummi Stick Dance	Remembers routine	☐
	Does not remember routine	☐

- -

EVALUATION

Area: Rhythms and Dance

Name _____ **Date of Observation** _____

Dance	Check one or more	
1. Alunelul	Changes directions with ease	☐
	Changes directions awkwardly	☐
2. Put Your Little Foot	Can perform mazurka step	☐
	Cannot perform mazurka step	☐
3. Lili Marlene	Can perform polka step	☐
	Cannot perform polka step	☐
4. Lummi Stick Dance	Remembers routine	☐
	Does not remember routine	☐

GATHERING PEASECODS ENGLAND

Basic Steps: Slide, walk, turn individually in place   4/4 time
Record: Victor LPM 1621
Formation: Four couples, single circle, all facing circle center. Girl on boy's right, all hands joined.

Steps		*Measures*
Part I	Slide 8 steps to the left.	**1-4**
	Drop hands and turn individually in place in 4 clockwise steps.	**5-6**
	Slide 8 steps to the right.	**7-10**
	Turn individually in place in 4 counterclockwise steps.	**11-12**
Chorus	While girls stand in place, boys join hands and slide 12 steps clockwise, returning to original position.	**13-18**
	Girls repeat measures 13-18 while boys stand in place.	**19-24**
	Boys walk 4 steps to center, right, left, right, left.	**25-26**
	Boys walk 4 steps back out; girls walk 4 steps to center.	**27-28**
	Girls walk 4 steps back out; boys walk 4 steps to center.	**29-30**
	Boys turn individually in place out to original position in 4 steps.	**31-32**
	Repeat the chorus with girls leading the movements.	

4

Part II	Face partner. Do-si-do in 8 walking steps.	**1-4**
	Turn individually in place.	**5-6**
	Repeat measures 1-6 (Part II).	**7-12**
	Repeat the chorus with girls leading the movements.	**13-32**
Part III	Hook right elbows and turn clockwise in 8 skipping steps.	**1-4**
	Turn individually in place.	**5-6**
	Repeat measures 1-6 (Part III), hooking left elbows.	**7-12**
	Repeat the chorus with boys leading the movements.	**13-32**

Related Activities:
- What is a peasecod?
- Where is England?
- What social customs and legal traditions have we borrowed or inherited from the English?

4

THE TWO-STEP   4/4 TIME

Directions:

In place: Side together, side, touch. Reverse.
Step to left, close right; step to left, touch right alongside.
Step to right, close left; step to right, touch left alongside.

Turning: Step remains the same as that done in place and may be done while turning either to the left or the right. To turn left, lead with the left foot. To turn right, lead with the right foot.

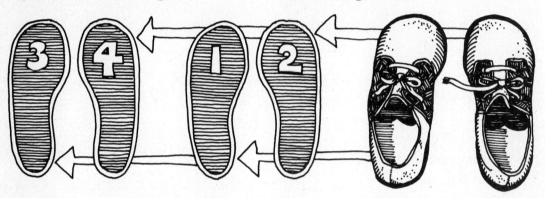

Two-step box: Side, together, forward, touch; side, together, back, touch.
Step to the left, close right; step forward left, touch right alongside (one-half box).
Step to the side with the right foot, close left; step back right, touch left alongside.
The box turn is easiest when quarter turns are used to start.

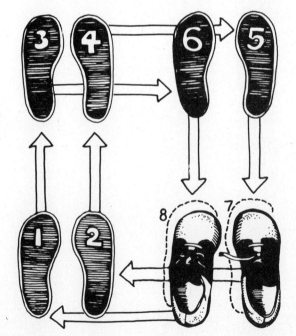

Note:
To teach the two-step, arrange all dancers in a line facing you, and use the opposite foot so that you move in the same direction they do even though you are facing them.

When the steps have been mastered, dancers can work with partners in social dance position and move freely following your cue or the boy's lead. For variation, the steps described above can be broken up with a simple walk.

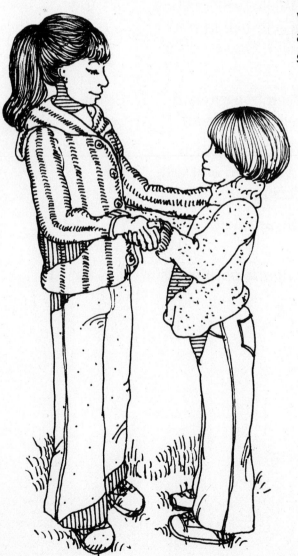

4

TEA FOR TWO   USA

Basic Step: Two-step   4/4 time
Record: Windsor 7606A
Formation: Double circle, couples facing counterclockwise, in
varsouvienne position, boy on inside.

Steps	*Measures*
Both starting on the left foot, do 2 two-steps forward.	**1-2**
Walk 4 steps forward, left, right, left, right.	**3-4**
Do 2 more two-steps forward, starting with the left foot.	**5-6**
Walk 4 steps, left, right, left, right. While walking, boy releases girl's left hand. Girl moves one-half turn around boy to end facing circle center. Boy pivots to face out from circle center.	**7-8**
Hold hands all around the circle. All move forward 1 two-step with left, backward 1 two-step with right.	**9-10**
Drop corner's hand, holding partner's, and switch positions, walking forward one-half circle to end with boys facing circle center and girls facing out.	**11-12**
All hold hands. Take 1 two-step forward (left), 1 two-step back (right).	**13-14**
In 4 walking steps, assume varsouvienne position with new partner (was your corner).	**15-16**

Repeat from beginning.

THE WALTZ   3/4 TIME

Directions:
Progressive waltz: **One**, two, three, **one**, two, three—either forward or backward.
Step forward left, bending knees slightly as this beat is accented. Take a small step forward right, small step forward left. These two steps are done slightly on the balls of the feet.

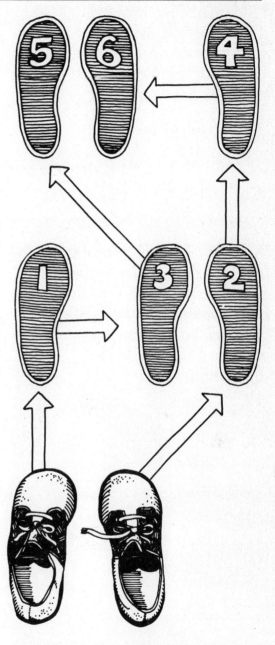

4

Note:
In teaching the waltz, remind dancers not to get carried away with the size of their steps: small steps are best. When steps are mastered, dancers can work with partners in social dance position and move freely around the floor. When working with partners, a balance step can be used as a first step to begin the waltz to help partners get in time with the music and each other.

Box waltz:

a. Step forward left, cut the corner. Step forward right to side of left, close left.

b. Step backward right, cut the corner. Step back to side of right, close right.

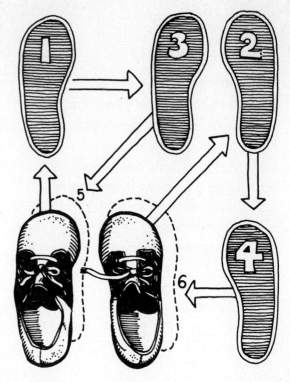

Box turn: The pivot for the turn is made on the forward or backward step. The boy leads outside girl's foot, stepping forward. Quarter turns will be best to begin. Use window or wall cues for orientation.

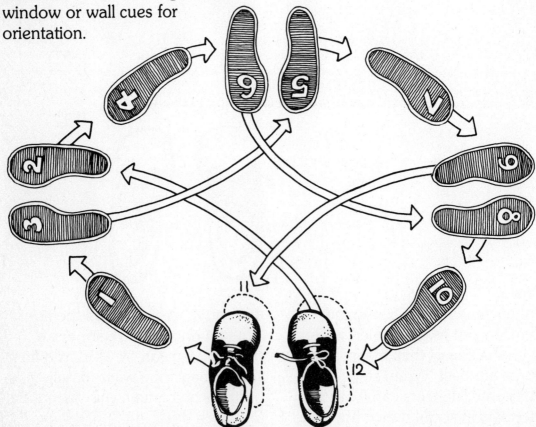

RYE WALTZ   USA

Basic Step: Point, walk, waltz   3/4 time
Records: MacGregor 298, Old Timer 8009, Imperial 1004, Folk Dancer
          3012
Formation: Double circle, partners facing and holding each other's
          hands, boys' backs to circle center.

Steps	*Measures*
Boy with left, girl with right, point to side and return.	**1-2**
Boy with right, girl with left, point to side and return.	**3-4**
Slide 3 times counterclockwise. Break hands, boys bow; girls curtsy.	**5-8**
Repeat measures 1-8, starting with opposite foot and sliding clockwise.	**9-16**
Take partner in social dance position and waltz in line of direction counterclockwise. The boy steps backward first so partners revolve clockwise as they move.	**17-32**

(*Variation:* Partners take varsouvienne position and waltz
in line of direction, both starting with inside foot.)

On last waltz step, turn partner under extended arm.
Girl progresses to next partner.

Repeat dance from the beginning.

Note:
It will take some practice to be able
to execute a turning waltz
smoothly. If it is too difficult, have
couples assume varsouvienne
position and do progressive waltz
to start.

4

HOT TIME   USA

Basic Steps: Walking
Records: Folkraft 1037, Windsor 7115
Square
Formation: Four couples standing in square; lady on gent's right.
Number off counterclockwise from couple with back to
music: 1, 2, 3, 4.

Steps

Introduction:
1. All join hands and circle left 8 steps.
2. Stop, hook right elbows with partner and turn once.
3. Walk in promenade position back to starting place ("home").

Figure:
1. First couple walk to couple 2; circle four.
2. Number 1 boy breaks hands, picks up couple 3, and continues to circle.
3. Number 1 boy breaks hands, picks up couple 4, and circles to home position.
4. Allemande left with corner (join left hands and make one circle with corner).
5. Pass partner (right shoulders). Allemande right (join right hands with girl past partner and walk all the way around once).
6. Pass partner. Allemande left with corner.
7. Grand right and left (give right hand to partner, left to next, right to next, left to next).
8. Meet partner and do-si-do (facing partner, pass right shoulders, pass back-to-back, pass left shoulders, and back away).
9. Hook right elbows with partner and turn once.
10. Promenade home.

Repeat figure three times, letting first couple 2, then couple 3, and finally couple 4 lead.

Finale:
1. Circle left 8 walking steps.
2. Hook right elbows with partner and swing.
3. Promenade home.

4

Additional Square Dances
The following are appropriate for this age and have easy-to-follow instructions with the music:

Take a Little Peek	Red River Valley
Birdie in the Cage	Oh Johnny
Forward Six	My Little Girl
Dive for the Oyster	Star by the Right

4

GRAND SQUARE   USA

Basic Step: Walk   4/4 time
Record: Perform to "Irish Washerwoman"
Formation: Square

Steps		*Measures*
Chorus	Moving in a square, couples 1 and 3 walk 4 steps toward each other. Face partner and *back* away 4 walking steps. Face gent/lady at side and back away 4 walking steps. Face partner and walk together 4 steps.	
	Moving in a square, couples 2 and 4 face partner and back away 4 walking steps. Face opposite lady/gent and walk 4 steps toward him/her. Face partner and walk 4 steps toward him/her. Pivot to stand at side of partner, facing opposite couple, and walk backward 4 steps to home.	
Chorus	Chorus.	**1-8**
	Chorus reverse.	**8-16**
Part I	Head ladies (1 and 3) chain across set (extend right hands to touch and pass), hook left elbows with opposite gent, and turn once around.	**1-4**
	Side ladies chain and hook elbows with opposite gent, turning once in place.	**5-8**
	Head ladies chain home, hook elbows, and turn.	**9-12**
	Side ladies chain home.	**13-16**
Chorus	Chorus.	**1-8**
	Chorus reverse.	**8-16**
Part II	Repeat Part I, with head gents then side gents chaining across the set to hook elbows and swing opposite lady, etc.	

Chorus	Chorus.	**1-8**
	Chorus reverse.	**8-16**
Part III	All ladies form right-hand star and walk in star formation halfway around set. Hook left elbows with opposite once around.	**1-8**
	Form right-hand star again and star home. Swing partner.	**8-16**
Chorus	Chorus.	**1-8**
	Chorus reverse.	**8-16**
Part IV	Men perform Part III, forming left-hand star, swinging opposite with right elbows, etc.	**1-16**
Chorus	Chorus.	**1-8**
	Chorus reverse.	**8-16**
Part V	All join hands, circle left halfway round.	**1-16**
	Take partner in promenade position and backtrack (move counterclockwise) home.	**1-16**
Chorus	Chorus.	**1-8**
	Chorus reverse.	**8-16**
Part VI	Grand right and left all the way around the square to home position.	**1-16**
Chorus	Chorus.	**1-8**
	Chorus reverse.	**8-16**

Note:

Chorus is repeated throughout dance. All couples move at the same time. Practice the chorus until all can perform easily as directed. To do chorus in reverse, backtrack the same steps and formation.

TINIKLING   PHILIPPINES

Basic Step: Hop   3/4 time
Record: RCA Victor LPM-1619
Equipment: Sets of bamboo poles (8 feet long and approximately 3 inches in diameter) resting on wood crossbars (2 inches x 2 inches x 2½ feet long). Acquire many sets so all can participate.
Formation: Sets of four; 2 dancers and 2 bangers at each set of poles. Partners face each other and hold both hands.

Bangers, holding poles about 15 inches apart, hit them twice against bars, then slide them together to tap them once. Bangers must practice well to be together and in time to music.

       1 measure = down, down, slide (return)

Dancers should practice basic steps hopping over poles held stationary or over ropes before ever trying to move through banging poles.

Steps		*Measures*
Part I	With left side to pole, touch toe between poles twice, then bend leg up and hold third count.	**1**
	Repeat measure 1 six times.	**2-7**
	Leading with the left foot, hop into middle of poles with left, hop into poles on right, hop out of poles with left to opposite side.	**8**
Part II	Repeat Part I, using opposite foot.	**1-8**
Part III	Repeat measure 8 (Part I), moving through poles leading first with left, then back with right.	**1-8**
Part IV	Partners move in opposite directions across poles. One does 1 touch step (measure 1, Part I), then 7 steps crossing back and forth. Other child starts with 7 steps moving back and forth across poles, then ends with 1 touch step.	**1-8**

Part V	Both partners jump into middle of poles on count 1, hop on both feet on count 2, and straddle the poles during the poles-close.	**1**
	Repeat measure 1, hopping twice in middle of poles then straddle.	**2-7**
	Hop twice in middle of poles then hop out of poles on third count (boys on right, girls on left) to end on starting side of poles.	**8**

Note:
Steps are described for boy; girl
does counterpart.

Related Activities:
* Many years ago there was a bird in the Philippine Islands called the tikling bird. A member of the crane family, this bird developed a strange habit of hopping so as not to get tangled in the undergrowth as it moved through the marshlands. The Philippine people, noticing this strange habit, created this dance in honor of the tikling bird.
* What unusual means of moving have other animals developed for survival?

OLD DOBBIN   USA

Basic Step: Shuffle walk   4/4 time
Music: The Old Grey Mare, She Ain't What She Used To Be
Formation: In this dance each couple imitates a horse. One child stands up straight and is the front half of the horse. The other child bends at the waist, places her hands on the waist of the front child, and keeping her back straight, places her head a few inches from the front child's waist, thus forming the rear half of the horse. A blanket around the front child and over the back of the other, plus a paper bag or papier mâché mask for the horse's head, creates "Old Dobbin," a crazy sort of animal whose front and rear halves seem to have minds of their own.

Steps		*Measures*
Part I	Starting with opposite feet, prance and/or shuffle walk in a circle or any pattern, following lead half of horse.	**1-32**
Part II	Both moving forward on right foot, prance 8 steps. Front half appears to stop after 8 steps while rear half keeps coming, running into front half. Front half looks around as if to find out what happened.	**32-40**
	Repeat measures 32-40 in reverse, moving backward. Rear half stops while front half does not.	**40-48**
Part III	Doing grapevine step sideways (step to right side with right foot, step left behind, step right to side, etc.), move 16 steps to right, rear half bending knees as if to sit, getting slowly closer and closer to floor.	**49-52**
	Reverse grapevine, moving to left. Front half now lowers as rear half straightens up.	**53-56**
	Repeat grapevine steps, first moving left, then right.	**57-64**

Part IV	Front half hops up and down 4 times. Rear half hops up and down 4 times.	**65-68**
	Front half looks around to right, and rear half moves to left as if to hide. Then reverse.	**69-72**
	Repeat measures 65-72.	**73-80**
Part V	Rear half circles forward in 8 running steps to stop with rear forward.	**81-84**
	Rear half sways right then left.	**85-86**
	Both dancers jump on both feet together, then rear kicks left foot to side while front kicks right foot to side. Repeat.	**87-88**
	Repeat measures 85-88 to end in original position.	**89-96**
Part VI	Repeat Part I, prancing in irregular patterns, rear half not keeping up with front and running into front when she pauses.	**96-128**
	End facing front crossing opposite legs (front, left over right; rear, right over left) to bow.	

EVALUATION

Area: Rhythms and Dance

Name _____ **Date of Observation** _____

Dance	Check one or more
1. Two-step	Can do basic step ☐ Can do box step ☐ Can do turning box ☐
2. Waltz	Can do progressive waltz ☐ Can do box waltz ☐ Can do turning box waltz ☐
3. Tinikling	Maintains balance ☐ Executes steps smoothly ☐

- -

Other Dances Suggested for This Level

Degree of Difficulty	Title	Record
Easy	Glow Worm Mixer Grand March Little Brown Jug Kalvelis	Folkraft E-1158 Columbia 52007, Folkraft 1304A Folk Dancer MH-1016B
Moderate	Ace of Diamonds Miserlou Gay Gordons	Victor 45-6169, 20989; Folkraft 1176 Columbia 7212, RCA Victor LPM-1620 Folkraft 1162
Advanced	Poi Poi ("Swinging Ball") Ba-O Dance (Philippine Coconut Dance) Varsouvienne	Koo-EE Poi Poi Twinson Company Educational Activities LP 520 Folkraft 1034, 1165

Record Sources

1. Eastern United States

Dance Record Center
1161 Broad Street
Newark, N.J. 07714

David McKay, Inc.
750 Third Avenue
New York, N.Y. 10017

Educational Activities, Inc.
P.O. Box 392
Freeport, N.Y. 11520

Educational Record Sales
157 Chambers Street
New York, N.Y. 10007

Folkraft Records
1159 Broad Street
Newark, N.J. 07714

Hoctor Educational Records, Inc.
Waldwick, N.J. 97463

Kimbo Educational Records
P.O. Box 246
Deal, N.J. 07723

Folk Dance House
108 W. 16th Street
New York, N.Y. 10011

Selva & Sons, Inc.
1607 Broadway
New York, N.Y. 10019

RCA Victor Education Department J
1133 Avenue of the Americas
New York, N.Y. 10036

2. Midwestern United States

Leo's Advance Theatrical Company
2451 N. Sacramento Avenue
Chicago, Ill. 60647

Loshin's
215 E. 8th Street
Cincinnati, Ohio 45202

Rhythm Record Company
9203 Nichols Road
Oklahoma City, Okla. 73120

3. Southern/ Southwestern United States

Record Center
2581 Piedmont Road N.E.
Atlanta, Ga. 30324

Merrback Records Service
P.O. Box 7308
Houston, Texas 77000

Cross Trail Square Dance Center
4150 S. W. 70th Court
Miami, Fla. 33155

4. Western United States

Rhythms Productions Records
Department J, Box 34485
Los Angeles, Calif. 90034

Russell Records
P.O. Box 3318
Ventura, Calif. 93003

Square Dance Square
P.O. Box 689
Santa Barbara, Calif. 93100

Standard Records & Hi Fi Company
1028 N. E. 65th
Seattle, Wash. 98115

Twinson Company
433 La Prenda Road
Los Altos, Calif. 94022

Children's Music Center
5373 W. Pico Blvd.
Los Angeles, Calif. 90019

Bowmar Records
4563 Colorado Blvd.
Los Angeles, Calif. 90039

Decker's Records
12425 Trent
Spokane, Wash. 99216

Master Record Service
708 East Garfield
Phoenix, Ariz. 85000

5. Canada

Canadian F.D.S. Educational Recordings
605 King Street
W. Toronto, 2B, Canada

STUNTS AND TUMBLING

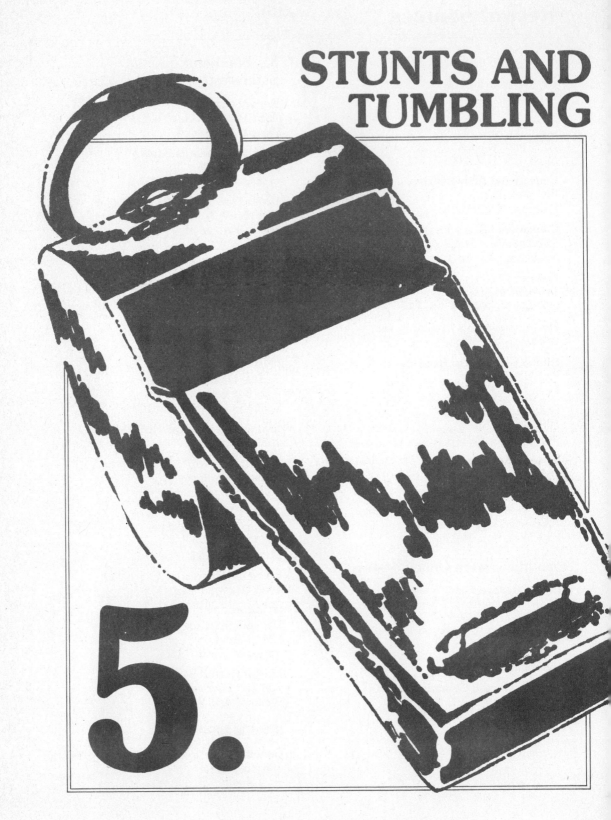

5.

This chapter covers exploration movements, simple stunts, and tumbling. The activities have been selected for eight- to twelve-year-old children. They require relatively small working areas and the following few items of equipment:

- balance beam (low)
- mats or thick blankets (folded)
- sponge bolster or thick blankets (rolled)

For children aged six through eight, the emphasis should be on exploring, experimenting, acquiring, and adapting a wide variety of skills as they practice the fundamentals of jumping, landing, supporting and shifting weight, curling, rolling, and body extension.

With children nine years old and older, attention should be given to developing control; increasing balance, coordination, and strength; and learning to perform patterns or set sequences of movements.

This chapter is divided into three sections. Each section begins with a list of warm-up activities. One or more of these should precede each skills learning session. Following each set of activities is an evaluation sheet for use in assessing skill attainment.

While stunts and tumbling activities generally involve familiar and creative movement, the actual skills may be new in both nature and physical orientation; therefore, children will not naturally progress from one activity to another without good instruction, adequate demonstration, and ample opportunity to practice. When first introduced, activities should be presented briefly. Tips on how to dress up a skill should be added later. Because children learn stunts and tumbling activities more by imitation than by verbal instruction, you should be prepared to demonstrate the activity, then let *everyone* try it. You might ask children who catch on quickly to provide additional demonstration as needed.

In stunts and tumbling activities, safety must be a prime consideration. Accidents are most likely to happen when children are pushed too quickly from one activity to another or when inadequate instruction is given. The best insurance against mishaps is provided by good instruction and demonstration, constant supervision, proper spotting techniques, and sufficient skill practice. Though activities are presented only once, they should be repeated several times so that individual skills can be mastered and perfected.

Consideration should also be given to clothing. Pants or shorts, tennis shoes *and socks* (shoes must be removed when working on mats), and comfortable shirts or tops allow children to move with ease and modesty.

During instruction and performance, children should be arranged so they can see and hear well, and move safely. Suggested formations are:

1. Well-spaced Lines

2. Free Formation

3. Semicircle

Possible mat formations include

5

81

WARM-UP ACTIVITIES (for pages 85-98)

1. JUMPING JACKS

- Stand with your feet together and your arms straight down at your sides.
- Jump to a straddle position (feet spread shoulder width), clapping your hands over your head.
- Jump a second time, bringing your feet back together and clapping your hands in front of your body.

Continue doing this two-count exercise: apart (clap), together (clap).

2. ALTERNATE TOE TOUCH

With your feet spread shoulder width and your arms extended straight out to the sides at shoulder height, bend at the waist to touch your right hand to your left foot, stand, then touch your left hand to your right foot. Repeat to a count of four: 1 (touch), 2 (stand), 3 (touch opposite), 4 (stand).

5

5

4. BALANCE TOUCH
Standing with your side to a drawn or painted line, balance on one foot and reach forward and across with your other foot to touch another line or marker (beanbag) on the *other* side of the first line. Maintaining your balance, touch only the object. Increase the distance to the object to be touched a little with each try.

3. STOOP AND STRETCH
Standing in well-spaced lines or a circle with your heels touching a painted or drawn line,
- Squat down with your feet apart.
- See how far back through your legs you can reach without losing your balance. Have someone mark your reach point.
- See how far around and through your legs you can reach. Have someone mark your reach point.

5. RELAY RACE
Use jumps, hops, leaps, and slides.

6. KNEE TOUCH

- While standing, bend your right (left) knee, raising your right (left) leg and grasping it at the ankle.

- Extending your left (right) arm for balance, slowly descend until you can touch your bent knee to the floor or ground.
- Ascend to your starting position. Your movement should be steady and smooth. If you lose your balance, let go of your ankle immediately.

7. TORSO TWIST

- Standing in place with your feet slightly apart and your arms extended straight out at shoulder level, twist your torso to the right, then to the left.
- Sitting on the floor or ground with your legs slightly apart and straight out in front of you and your arms extended straight out at shoulder level, twist your torso to the right, then to the left.
- Repeat in a sitting position with your legs crossed.

5

CRANE DIVE

5 MIN.

Purpose: Developing strength, balance, flexibility
Equipment: None
Play Area: Clean, flat, smooth surface in a classroom (cleared), gym, or yard
Formation: Well-spaced lines.

Directions:
- With your weight on one foot and your arms extended back along your torso for balance, lift the other leg backward.
- Keeping both legs as straight as possible and your eyes forward, slowly lean forward as far as you can without losing your balance.
- Vary the position of your arms, or see if you can pick up a small object off the floor.

Related Activities:
- Talk about cranes: What is a crane? Where do cranes live? What do they eat? What size (how tall) are they? How long are their legs?
- Can you *crane* your neck?
- What kind of bird is a *rail*?
- What are stilts? If some are available, try them out.

5

BALANCE AND REVERSE   5 MIN.

Purpose: Developing balance, strength
Equipment: None
Play Area: Clean, flat, *smooth* surface in a classroom, gym, or yard
Formation: Well-spaced lines or free formation.

Directions:

- Standing with your weight on your right (left) foot, bend forward at the waist, extending your arms out to the sides and your left (right) foot backward.

- Swing your left (right) foot down and forward, twisting it in and turning it over so that the knee points down. Use the momentum gained thereby to swing your body around to face in the opposite direction.

Note:

Movement is accomplished by pivoting on supporting foot. Swinging foot does *not* touch the ground.

5

COFFEE GRINDER   5 MIN.

Purpose: Developing strength, balance
Equipment: None
Play Area: Clean, flat, smooth surface in a classroom (cleared), gym, or yard
Formation: Well-spaced lines.

Directions:

- Sit with your legs out straight in front of you and your hands, palms down, on the floor behind your hips.
- Roll to one side and raise your hips off the floor, supporting your weight on the hand and foot nearest the floor or ground.
- Taking small "steps" with your feet, pivot on the supporting arm, keeping it straight.
- Repeat the activity on the opposite side.
- Vary the speed of your turn.

Related Activities:

- Talk about coffee: From what is it made? Where are the beans grown? How are they processed?
- What other foods are processed by grinding?
- What implements did people of long ago use to do their grinding?
- Talk about balance: What is it? What part do your eyes, ears, and the small bones in your feet play in maintaining it.
- Why might recurrent dizziness be one sign of an inner ear infection?

5

FALLING   10 MIN.

Purpose: Developing lead-up skills, agility, spatial awareness
Equipment: Mats or thick blankets (folded)
Play Area: Gym, cleared classroom, or yard
Formation: Mats in well-spaced lines or a semicircle with children
alongside.

Directions:
- Stand to the side of the mat.
- Fold your arms across your chest.
- Bend your knees slightly.
- Roll onto the mat, landing on the outside of your knee, on the side of your hip, and on your shoulder.

Note:
Be sure to have children keep their arms folded and out of the way.

Related Activities:
- Talk about the importance of rolling with a fall, keeping your hands and arms out of the way, and landing on your side.
- If possible observe, in movies, on television, or by visiting a movie studio, how professional stunt men take their falls. Thanks to television's "instant replay," children may be able to see this same technique used by professional football players and other athletes.

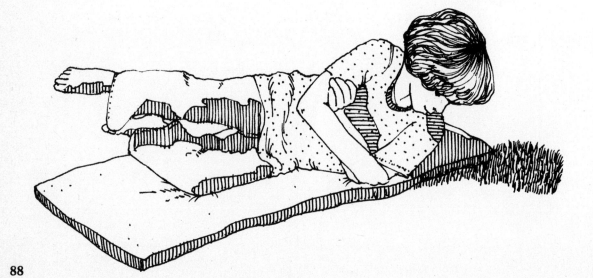

FORWARD ROLL   15 MIN.

Purpose: General conditioning; developing agility, spatial awareness
Equipment: Mats or thick blankets (folded)
Play Area: Clean, flat, smooth surface in a classroom (cleared), gym, or yard
Formation: Children in 1 or 2 lines facing mats (2 or 3) placed end-to-end. Be prepared to spot each child during his first few attempts to do this activity.

Directions:
- With your feet apart, squat down and place your hands flat on the mat.
- Tuck your head between your knees.
- Springing slightly to transfer your weight from your feet to your hands, roll forward in a tuck position.
- As your weight is transferred from your hands to the nape of your neck and then to your back, bring your hands forward to clasp your shins.
- Continue rolling until your feet are under you, then stand.
- Vary by doing continuous rolls (do not stand in between) or by rolling with your legs crossed.

Note:
The nape of the neck, not the head, should touch the mat first. If a child is rolling over one shoulder, suggest he spread his feet farther apart, distribute his weight evenly on both, and push off equally with both.

To Spot:
"Lift" and push in the direction of the roll at the nape of the neck and at the shin.

5

See illustration on page 90.   89

Forward Roll

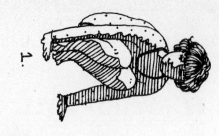

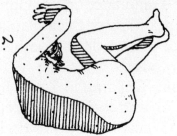

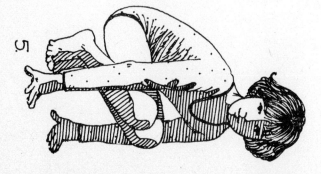

HUMAN BALL   5 MIN.

Purpose: Developing agility, spatial awareness
Equipment: Mats or thick blankets (folded)
Play Area: Clean, flat, smooth surface in a classroom (cleared), gym, or yard
Formation: Children on mats arranged in well-spaced lines or a semicircle.

Directions:

- Sitting with your knees bent and your ankles crossed, extend your arms *under* your knees and *inside* your legs, to grasp your right ankle with your right hand, your left ankle with your left hand.
- Rock to the right (left) then roll to the left (right) over your knee to your shoulder, your back, your other shoulder, and back to a sitting position.

Related Activities:

- Talk about the safety aspects of rolling with a fall.
- For additional activity suggestions, see Falling, page 88.

5

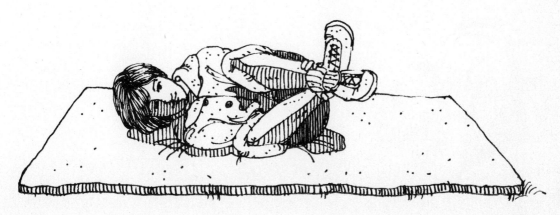

BICYCLING   5 MIN.

Purpose: General conditioning; developing strength, flexibility, and balance
Equipment: 1 mat or thick blanket (folded) for each child
Play Area: Classroom (cleared), gym, or yard
Formation: Children well spaced, lying on mats with arms at sides; all facing one direction.

Directions:

- Raise your legs and body to a vertical position so that your weight is supported on your neck, shoulders, and arms.
- Bend your arms up at the elbows and rest your hips in your hands.
- Bend your knees, and rotate your legs as if you are pedaling a bicycle.
- Vary your speed: pedal faster, slower; push hard as if you are climbing a steep hill.

Related Activities:

- Talk about bike safety. Include a demonstration of correct hand signals.
- Stage a "bicycle rodeo" in which bicycles are inspected for safety features (headlamp, horn, reflectors), bicycle owners are tested for their knowledge of traffic laws as they apply to riding a bicycle, and cyclists ride over a course designed so that they must demonstrate their ability to handle the cycle and their knowledge and use of hand signals.

UP AND OVER   10 MIN.

Purpose: General conditioning; developing strength, flexibility, balance
Equipment: 1 mat or thick blanket (folded) for each child
Play Area: Classroom (cleared), gym, or yard
Formation: Children well-spaced, lying on mats, all facing one direction.

Directions:
- Put your arms straight along your sides, palms to the mat, to push and use for balance.
- Keeping your knees straight, raise your legs together slowly, and touch your toes to the mat above your head. (To do this activity properly, you will have to lift your back off the mat, transferring your weight to your neck, shoulders, and arms.)
- Slowly return to your starting position.
- Repeat to an even count.

TRIPOD TIP-UP   10 MIN.

Purpose: Developing strength, flexibility, balance
Equipment: 1 mat or thick blanket (folded) for each child
Play Area: Classroom (cleared), gym, or yard
Formation: Children on mats arranged in well-spaced lines or a
          semicircle.

Directions:

Tripod

- Imagine a triangle drawn on your mat such that its base is the width of your shoulders.
- Place your *hairline* at the apex and your hands (palms down, fingers pointing forward) at the base corners.
- Lift your hips high by "walking" your feet toward your hands.
- Place your right knee on your right elbow; place your left knee on your left elbow.
- Hold this position.
- Return to original position *slowly* by first taking down one knee and then the other, and reversing your walking action.

- Without letting your head touch the mat, continue leaning forward until your feet are off the ground.
- Hold.
- Reverse, slowly transferring your weight back to your feet to finish.

Tip-up

- Squat with your knees spread, your arms between your knees, your hands on the mat a shoulders' width apart.
- As you transfer your weight forward from your feet to your hands, bend your elbows and push them against your bent knees.

5

JUMP FROM KNEES   10 MIN.

Purpose: Developing strength, flexibility
Equipment: 1 mat or thick blanket (folded) per child
Play Area: Clean, flat, smooth surface in a classroom (cleared), gym, or yard
Formation: On mats in well-spaced lines or semicircle.

Directions:

- Kneel on your mat with your weight on your knees-shins-feet, your back straight, and your body erect.
- Swing your arms forward and up, using the momentum of your arm swing to lift your body to your feet and then on up to a standing position.

Note:

Swinging arms up and overhead will provide momentum; arm movement should be forward and up, not backward.

Related Activities:

- Talk about *momentum*.
- If two vehicles of *different* weights are traveling side by side along the same road at the same speed and the drivers apply their brakes at the same instant, will they both stop in the same amount of time and at the same spot in the road? Discuss.

5

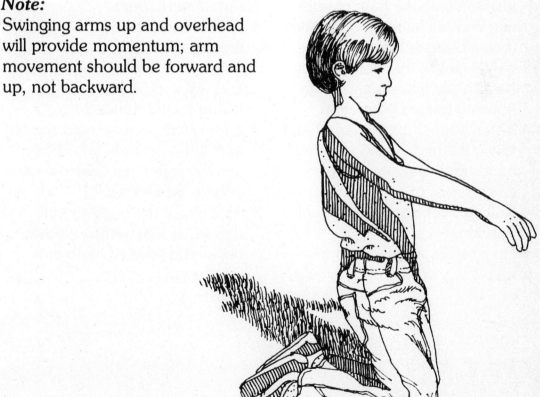

BACKWARD ROLL   15 MIN.

Purpose: Developing strength, flexibility
Equipment: Mats or thick blankets (folded)
Play Area: Clean, flat, smooth surface in a classroom (cleared), gym, or yard
Formation: In 1 or 2 lines facing mats placed end-to-end. Have each child turn his back to the mat and stand with his heels against the edge to ensure room for movement.

Directions:

- Squat with your back to the mat and your heels against its edge, placing your hands (palms down, thumbs in) on the floor at shoulder width.
- Tuck your head between your knees.
- Remaining in a tuck position, push off with the balls of your feet and roll backward, bending your elbows and bringing your hands, palms up, alongside your head. Your thumbs should be pointing toward your ears.
- When your shoulders and head touch the mat, push with your hands and straighten your elbows.
- Roll on over to end in a squat position.
- Do a series of rolls down the mats.

To Spot:

- As a child rolls and his hips come up in the air, grasp them and lift to guide the roll and lighten the load on his neck.
- Watch that each child maintains a tuck position and lifts with his arms.

Related Activities:

- Talk about the body, especially those parts that are weak or vulnerable to pressure or blows, and ways to protect it (e.g., letting your extended arms—with elbows held straight and stiff—precede your body into the water in a dive to protect your head and neck.)
- Talk about the body's joints (knees, ankles, wrists, elbows, neck) and their strength and weakness.

5

PARTNER HOP   5 MIN.

Purpose: Developing balance, agility
Equipment: None
Play Area: Classroom (cleared), gym, or yard
Formation: Well-spaced, free formation with partner pairs facing each
other.

Directions:
- Extend your left (right) leg forward.
- Grasp your partner's left (right) ankle with your right (left) hand.
- Take small hops on your right (left) leg in first one direction, then another.

Variations:
- Stand back-to-back, lift your leg backward, grasp your partner's leg at the ankle, and hop.
- Stand side-to-side, put your inside arm around your partner's waist, lift your inside foot, and hop.

Note:
Partners should be about the same height. If your partner loses his balance, let go of his ankle immediately.

BALANCE BEAM ACTIVITIES

Purpose: Developing balance

Equipment: Line taped or drawn on the floor; low balance beam. The latter can be a simple wood plank resting on the floor but secured so that it does not rock or tip.

Play Area: Classroom (cleared), gym, or yard

Formation: Single-file line facing one end of the painted line or balance beam.

Directions:

On a line taped or drawn on the floor,

- walk heel-to-toe, extending your arms to your sides for balance. Keep your back straight and your eyes ahead, not down.

On the balance beam,

- walk heel-to-toe slowly from one end to the other, extending your arms for balance.
- walk half way across, stop, slowly descend into a deep knee bend, rise, and continue walking forward to the far end of the beam.
- walk half way across, turn by pivoting on the balls of both feet, and return to your starting point.
- hop from one end to the other. Remember to let your knees give (bend) as you land.

Related Activities:

What is *symmetry*? Where do you see it? How does it affect balance?

5

EVALUATION

Area: Stunts and Tumbling

Name _____ **Date of Observation** _____

Stunt	Check one or more
1. Crane Dive	Movements are smooth ☐ Movements are jerky ☐ Maintains balance ☐ Cannot maintain balance ☐
2. Coffee Grinder	Can perform stunt with weight on right hand ☐ Can perform stunt with weight on left hand ☐
3. Forward Roll	Maintains tuck position ☐ Nape of neck touches mat first ☐ Completes stunt in standing position ☐
4. Backward Roll	Maintains tuck position ☐ Straightens arms to take weight off neck ☐

Additional comments:

WARM-UP ACTIVITIES (for pages 102-112)

1. COFFEE GRINDER

- Sit with your legs out straight in front of you and your hands, palms down, on the floor behind your hips.
- Roll to one side and raise your hips off the floor, supporting your weight on the hand and foot nearest the floor or ground.
- Taking small "steps" on the sides of your feet, pivot on your supporting arm, keeping it straight.
- Repeat this activity on the opposite side.
- Vary the speed of your turn.

2. BICYCLING

- Lying on a mat or thick blanket with your arms at your side, raise your legs and body to a vertical position so that your weight is supported on your neck, shoulders, and arms.
- Bend your arms up at the elbows and rest your hips in your hands.
- Bend your knees, and rotate your legs as if you are pedaling a bicycle.
- Vary your speed: pedal faster, slower; push hard as if you are climbing a steep hill.

3. BALANCE BEAM ACTIVITIES

On a line taped or drawn on the floor or a low balance beam,

- walk heel-to-toe slowly from one end to the other, extending your arms to your sides for balance. Keep your back straight and your eyes ahead, not down.
- walk half way across, stop, slowly descend into a deep knee bend, rise, and continue walking forward to the far end of the beam.
- walk half way across, turn by pivoting on the balls of your feet, and return to your starting point.
- hop from one end to the other, remembering to let your knee give (bend) as you land.

5

4. TREADMILL

- Bend your knees and assume a squat position.
- Lean forward and place your hands flat on the floor or ground below your shoulders with your fingers pointing forward.
- Extend your left leg straight out behind you, placing the sole of your left foot on the floor or ground.

- Rocking slightly forward to place your weight temporarily on your arms, exchange the positions of your legs (draw up the left, extend the right) with a jumping motion.
- Repeat the exercise rhythmically to a count or music.

5. RUNNING IN PLACE

Standing well spaced, run in place, swinging your arms, varying your speed, and lifting your knees to your chest.

6. CIRCLES

Standing in place with your feet slightly apart for balance, make large or small circles (as directed) with your hands, arms, head, torso, left foot, left leg, right foot, right leg, or a combination of these. Do the leg circles to the front, lifting your leg off the floor and extending your arms to your sides for balance.

TRIPOD HEADSTAND   15 MIN.

Purpose: Developing strength, coordination, balance
Equipment: Mats or thick blankets (folded)
Play Area: Classroom (cleared), gym, or yard
Formation: In lines facing well-spaced mats. Use the same number of lines as there are spotters available. Spotter stands in front of and facing the performer.

Directions:
- Assume a tripod position with your head and hands on the mat.
- Slowly lift your legs and extend them, straightening your knees, to assume headstand position.
- Hold briefly.

Note:
In assuming the tripod position, place your hands on the mat just in front of your knees and your head the length of your forearm away from each knee. If you lose your balance, tuck into a forward roll.

To Spot:
Stand in front of and facing the performer. As he assumes the tripod position, support his hips. As his legs are extended, reach up to support them by grasping his ankles. If he loses his balance, step out of his direct line of roll.

5

HEADSTAND KICK-UP   15 MIN.

Purpose: Developing strength, coordination, balance
Equipment: Mats or thick blankets (folded)
Play Area: Classroom (cleared), gym, or yard
Formation: In lines facing well-spaced mats. Use half as many lines as
there are spotters available: each performer should have
two spotters, one kneeling on either side.

Directions:

- Assume a tripod position with your head and hands on the mat and your knees on the floor.
- Kick up and extend one leg then the other in a quick, steady one-two movement.
- Hold briefly.

Note:

Do not hold this position very long. If you loose your balance, tuck into a forward roll.

To Spot:

Kneel at performer's side, placing one hand under his shoulder. As he kicks up, reach up to grasp his leg nearest you with your other hand.

5

103

DOUBLE FORWARD ROLL   10 MIN.

Purpose: Developing strength, coordination
Equipment: Mats or thick blankets (folded)
Play Area: Classroom (cleared), gym, or yard
Formation: In lines facing mats (2 or 3) placed end-to-end. Children
work in pairs.

Directions:
- One child lies on the mat facing up.
- The other child stands, straddling the first child's head.
- Each child grasps the other's ankles.
- The standing child initiates the forward roll.

Note:
Children should tuck their heads so that they roll first on the nape of the neck, then on the shoulders. This stunt works best if partners are of the same size.

5

RUSSIAN DANCE   10 MIN.

Purpose: Developing strength, coordination
Equipment: Mats or thick blankets (folded)
Play Area: Classroom (cleared), gym, or yard
Formation: Well-spaced formation on mats or floor.

Directions:

Step 1
- Squat with your hands touching the floor or ground and your knees together.
- Spring up to a standing position, spreading your legs, putting your weight on your heels, and extending your arms to the sides for balance.
- Return to squat position.
- Perform to a rhythmic count: down, up; down, up; 1, 2, 3, 4.

Step 2
- Squat down, sitting on one heel with your weight on the ball of that same foot.
- Extend your other leg forward and hold your arms out for balance.
- Keeping your back straight, rapidly exchange the position of your legs. Your weight should be supported by the bent leg and the heel of the extended leg.
- Perform to an even, rhythmic count at medium speed.
- Vary by changing the position of your arms (cross them over your chest) and hands (place them on your hips).

Related Activities:
- Show a film of Russian or Ukrainian dancers performing. Note their costumes and their strength and gymnastic ability.
- Attend a ballet performance. Note the grace and strength of the dancers. Discuss the story on which the dance is based and the composer who wrote the music.

5

105

SKIN THE SNAKE   10 MIN.

Purpose: Developing coordination, flexibility
Equipment: Mats or thick blankets (folded)
Play Area: Classroom (cleared), gym, or yard
Formation: Single-file lines of 8 to 10 children at one end of mats placed end-to-end. Allow 20 feet of mat for stunt.

Directions:

- First child stands facing the extended mat with his feet at its edge.
- Bending down, he reaches between his legs with his right hand to grasp the left hand of the person behind him.
- Continuing to hold hands, he does a forward roll onto the mat, ending flat on his back with his feet spread.
- Second child moves forward to straddle the head of the first, reaches between his legs to grasp the hand of the child behind him, and completes his roll in the same position.
- When all have completed the roll and are lying on the mat, hands joined right to left, the person who rolled first stands up and all others follow his lead. Together they walk forward several steps with their hands still joined.

Related Activities:

- Talk about snakes: Name several different kinds or types of snakes. Talk about what and how snakes eat. Point out that not all snakes are poisonous and discuss how to identify readily and avoid those in your area that are.
- Are snakes good or bad? Discuss.
- If possible, view snakes on display at a zoo or pet store, or have children bring pet ones from home. If the latter, talk about what qualities in snakes make them good pets and how to care for them properly.
- Why does a snake shed its skin? What other reptiles shed their skins?
- What is an *asp*?

5

DIVE ROLL   10 MIN.

Purpose: Developing coordination, flexibility
Equipment: Mats or thick blankets (folded); sponge bolster or blankets (rolled)
Play Area: Classroom (cleared), gym, or yard
Formation: Well-spaced single-file line facing mat. Place bolster or rolled blankets at mat end nearest children.

Directions:
- Standing at the edge of the mat, lean forward until your hands are flat on the mat on the other side of the bolster.
- Extend your feet to the rear, keeping your legs straight and your hips high.
- Push off with your feet, tucking your head such that the nape of your neck and your shoulders touch the mat first on the *far* side of the bolster.
- Roll rapidly in a tuck position to stand.

Variations:
- Back up and, taking several steps, spring forward into a roll with or without the bolster.

Note:
The nape of the neck, not the head, should touch the mat first. Tuck position should be taken during the roll with hands on knees or grasping shins. If children have difficulty with this activity, practice forward rolls.

5

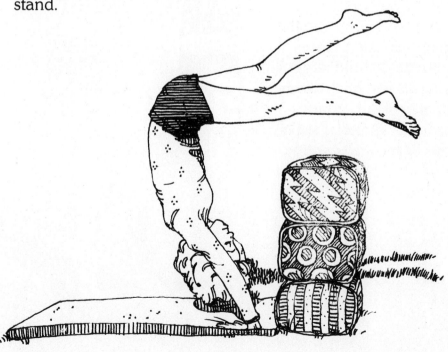

PARTNER HANDSTAND   10 MIN.

Purpose: Developing strength, balance, coordination.
Equipment: Mats or thick blankets (folded)
Play Area: Classroom (cleared), gym, or yard
Formation: In facing pairs on mats placed in well-spaced lines or semicircle.

Directions:

- Partners stand 3 or 4 feet apart facing each other.
- One bends down, places his hands on the ground, and slowly brings his feet up over his head, keeping his elbows straight and balancing his weight on his hands.
- The other grasps the ankles of the first to help him find and hold his balance.
- Exchange roles so that second partner does handstand and first partner spots.

Note:

If partner doing handstand loses his balance, spotter should let go so he can bring his feet back down to their original position or tuck into a forward roll. Spotter should step out of his direct line of roll.

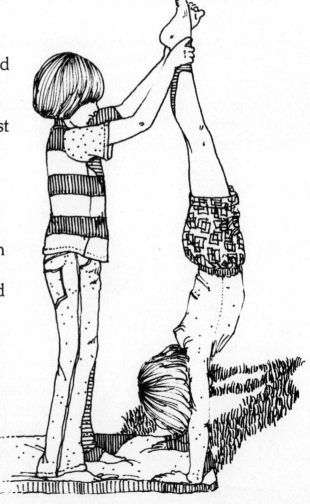

HANDSTAND

10 MIN.

Purpose: Developing strength, balance, coordination
Equipment: Mats or thick blankets (folded)
Play Area: Classroom (cleared), gym, or yard
Formation: In facing pairs on mats placed in well-spaced lines or semicircle.

Directions:

- When either partner can execute handstand smoothly, spotting partner backs away after balance is achieved.
- Partner doing handstand should look at the floor and arch his back slightly to maintain balance.
- If balance is lost, partner doing handstand should bring his feet back down to their original position or tuck into a forward roll. Spotting partner should step out of his direct line of roll.

Variation: Spread Eagle Handstand

- Work in groups of three standing side-by-side with middle child facing the opposite direction.
- On count, the middle child bends and lifts to a handstand.
- Each outside member of threesome grasps the ankle nearest her with her inside hand.
- Hold.
- Slowly lower legs to complete.

Related Activities:

Talk about posture as a way of properly distributing and carrying the body's weight. Stress the importance of correct vertical alignment in standing and sitting. Use the section in Chapter 9 for ideas.

5

MONKEY ROLL

10 MIN.

Purpose: Developing coordination, balance, timing
Equipment: Mats or thick blankets (folded)
Play Area: Classroom (cleared), gym, or yard
Formation: Work in groups of three. All three should be on their hands and knees about 3 feet apart on the mat facing the same direction.

Directions:

- Middle child lowers her body and rolls to the right.
- Child on the right dives left over rolling middle child to center position on mat and rolls to the left.
- Child on the left dives right over rolling child from right and stops in middle.
- Repeat.

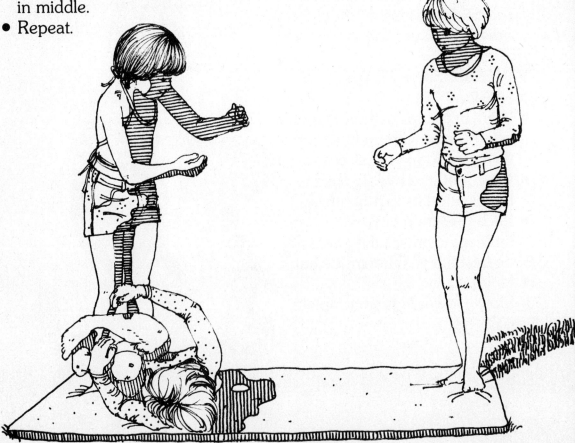

SIX-LEGGED ANIMAL   10 MIN.

Purpose: Developing coordination, balance, timing
Equipment: Mats or thick blankets (folded)
Play Area: Classroom (cleared), gym, or yard
Formation: Well-spaced lines or free formation; all moving in the same direction. Children work in pairs facing the same direction.

Directions:

- Partner 1 kneels on all fours.
- Partner 2 sits astride partner 1's back.
- Partner 2 leans forward to take his weight on his own hands, which he places 1 to 2 feet in front of partner 2's hands, and hooks his feet together under partner 1's chest.
- Partners walk slowly forward and backward in this position.
- Change positions so that partner 2 is on all fours with partner 1 astride.

5

ROOSTER FIGHT   5 MIN.

Purpose: Developing coordination, balance, timing
Equipment: Mats or thick blankets (folded)
Play Area: Classroom (cleared), gym, or yard
Formation: Well-spaced free formation with children in pairs. Establish boundaries for each pair.

Directions:

- Fold your arms across your chest, lift one foot, and balance on the other.
- Hop about, bumping shoulders with your partner until you make her lose her balance and unfold her arms or put her foot down to regain it.

Note:
Do not allow children to throw body blocks or otherwise become excessively rough. Gentle shoulder bumps and nudges are all that is required.

5

EVALUATION

Area: Stunts and Tumbling

Name _____ **Date of Observation** _____

Stunt	Check one or more
1. Tripod Headstand	Movements are smooth ☐ Achieves balance ☐ Can assume position and tuck to forward roll ☐
2. Headstand Kick-up	Movements are smooth ☐ Achieves balance ☐ Can assume position and tuck to forward roll ☐
3. Dive Roll	Shoulders touch mat first ☐ Achieves tuck position on roll ☐
4. Handstand with Spotter	Spotter assumes correct position ☐ Performer achieves balance ☐ Performer can tuck into forward roll to compensate for loss of balance ☐

Additional comments:

5

WARM-UP ACTIVITIES (for pages 117-126)

1.   JUMPING JACKS
- Stand with your feet together and your arms straight down at your sides.
- Jump to a straddle position (feet spread shoulder width), clapping your hands over your head.
- Jump a second time, bringing your feet back together and clapping your hands in front of your body.

Continue doing this two-count exercise: apart (clap), together (clap).

2.   RUNNING IN PLACE
Standing well spaced, run in place, swinging your arms, varying your speed, and lifting your knees to your chest.

3.   ALTERNATE TOE TOUCH
With your feet spread shoulder width and your arms extended straight out to the sides at shoulder height, bend at the waist to touch your right hand to your left foot, stand, then touch your left hand to your right foot. Repeat to a count of four: 1 (touch), 2 (stand), 3 (touch opposite), 4 (stand).

4.   TORSO TWIST
- Standing in place with your feet slightly apart and your arms extended straight out at shoulder level, twist your torso to the right, then to the left.
- Sitting on the floor or ground with your legs slightly apart and straight out in front of you and your arms extended straight out at shoulder level, twist your torso to the right, then to the left.
- Repeat in sitting position with your legs crossed.

5

5. CONTINUOUS FORWARD ROLL

- With your feet apart, squat down and place your hands flat on the mat.
- Tuck your head between your knees.
- Springing slightly to transfer your weight from your feet to your hands, roll forward in a tuck position.
- As your weight is transferred from your hands to the nape of your neck and then to your shoulders and back, bring your hands forward to clasp your shins.
- Continue rolling until your feet are under you, then roll again. Do not stand between rolls.

6. CRANE DIVE

With your weight on one foot, your other foot extended to the rear, your arms along your sides, and your eyes looking forward, bend forward *slowly* and maintain for a count of 5. *Slowly* pick up a small object from the floor. Repeat.

7. BALANCE AND REVERSE

- Standing with your weight on your right (left) foot, bend forward at the waist, extending your arms out to the sides and your left (right) foot backward.
- Swing your left (right) foot down and forward, twisting it in and turning it over so that the knee points down. Use the momentum gained thereby to swing your body around to face in the opposite direction.

Movement is accomplished by pivoting on supporting foot. Swinging foot should not touch the ground.

5

8. RUSSIAN DANCE

Step 1

- Squat with your hands touching the floor or ground and your knees together.
- Spring up to a standing position, putting your weight on your heels, and extending your arms to the sides for balance.
- Return to squat position.
- Perform to a rhythmic count: down, up; down, up; 1, 2, 3, 4.

Step 2

- Squat down, sitting on one heel with your weight on the ball of that same foot.
- Extend your other leg forward and hold your arms out for balance.
- Keeping your back straight, rapidly exchange the position of your legs. Your weight should be supported by the bent leg and the heel of the extended leg.
- Perform to an even, rhythmic count at medium speed.
- Vary by changing the position of your arms (cross them over your chest) and hands (place them on your hips).

5

THE BRIDGE   5 MIN.

Purpose: Developing strength, balance
Equipment: 1 mat or thick blanket (folded) for each child
Play Area: Classroom (cleared), gym, or yard
Formation: Lying supine on individual mats arranged in well-spaced lines or semicircle.

Directions:
- Lying supine on your mat, bend your knees and place your feet on the mat near your buttocks.
- Put your hands, palms down, under your hips.
- Pushing with your hands, raise your hips high into the air.
- Now lift your hands so that your body is supported on your feet and head.

Related Activities:
- What do *prone* and *supine* mean?
- Talk about bridges. What different types and sizes do you know about? Learn about some others. Where is the longest bridge? The tallest?

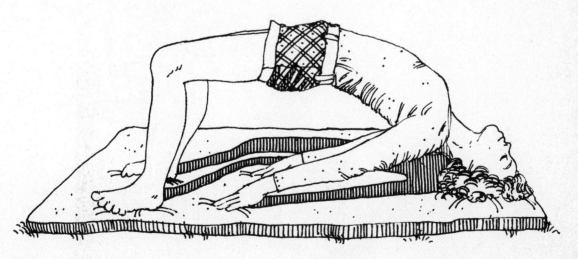

BASE OF SUPPORT   1 MIN.

Purpose: Developing strength, balance
Equipment: 1 mat or thick blanket (folded) for every two children
Play Area: Classroom (cleared), gym, or yard
Formation: Partner pairs on mats arranged in well-spaced lines or semicircle.

Directions:
See how many ways you and your partner can balance together. Start with many (7 or 8) points (hands, feet, knees, buttocks) touching the ground and decrease the number one at a time.

Related Activities:
- Talk about the importance of the base of support or foundation.
- What is *stability*? How stable is a three-legged stool?

5

TURNOVER   5 MIN.

Purpose: Developing strength, balance
Equipment: 1 mat or thick blanket (folded) per each child
Play Area: Classroom (cleared), gym, or yard
Formation: Lying supine on mats arranged in well-spaced lines or
semicircle or placed end-to-end (for continuous turnover).

Directions:

- Lying on your back, draw your feet up close to your buttocks.
- Bend your elbows and place your hands (palms down, fingers pointing toward your feet) next to your head.
- Push up with your legs and arms, lifting your hips so your body is level from the knees to the neck.
- Swing your right (left) arm and leg over so that you end up facing down, rather than up.
- Swing your right (left) arm and leg back so that you face up once again.
- Perform a series of continuous turnovers.

5

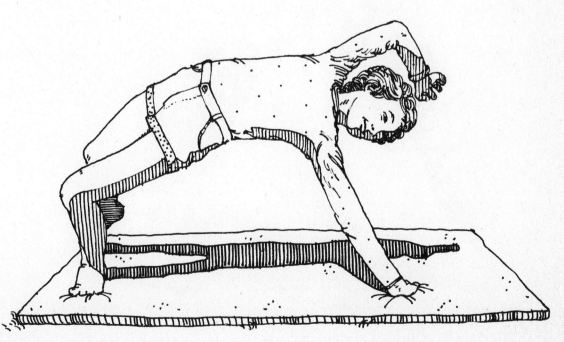

119

PUSH AND CLAP   5 MIN.

Purpose: Developing balance, agility
Equipment: None
Play Area: Clean, flat, smooth area in a classroom (cleared), gym, or yard
Formation: Well-spaced lines, semicircle, or free formation. Partner pairs stand 3 feet apart facing each other.

Directions:
- Spread your feet slightly.
- Raising both of your hands, clap and push them against your partner's in an effort to force her to move one of her feet.

Note:
Partners should be of approximately equal height and weight. Caution against unnecessary roughness.

5

MERRY-GO-ROUND   10 MIN.

Purpose: Developing agility, balance
Equipment: None
Play Area: Clean, flat, *smooth* area in a classroom (cleared), gym, or yard
Formation: Small circles of 8 children each. Leave plenty of room between circles. Have circle members number off by twos: one, two, one, two.

Directions:

- Ones lie in a circle with their feet touching in the center.
- Twos tightly grasp the nearest wrists of ones.
- As twos take small steps sideways, ones keep their bodies straight and are carried around, pivoting on their heels.
- Exchange positions so that twos lie in a circle and are carried around by ones.

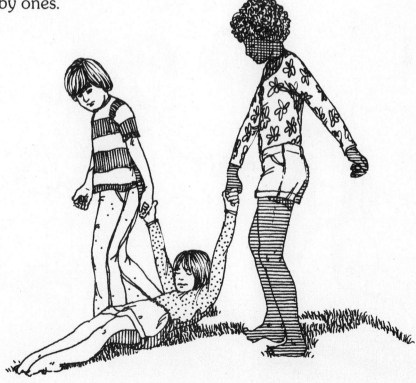

5

ONE-ARM WRESTLE   5 MIN.

Purpose: Developing agility, balance
Equipment: None
Play Area: Clean, flat, smooth area in a classroom (cleared), gym, or yard
Formation: Well-spaced lines, semicircle, or free formation. Partner pairs stand facing each other.

Directions:

- Grasp your partner's right hand with your right hand.
- Raise your left foot.
- Push and pull, attempting to force your partner to move her right foot or put her left foot down.

Related Activities:

Talk about the push and pull action of *synergist* and *antagonist* muscle sets in the body. Use the section in Chapter 9 and the poster for ideas.

Note:

Partners should be of approximately the same height and weight.

5

BACKWARD EXTENSION ROLL 30 MIN.

Purpose: Developing strength, coordination
Equipment: Mats or thick blankets (folded)
Play Area: Classroom (cleared), gym, or yard
Formation: Single-file lines, backed up to mats (2 or 3) placed end-to-end. Be prepared to spot each child during his first few attempts to do this activity.

Directions:

Before beginning this activity, review the backward roll, then
- Squat with your heels against the edge of the mat, placing your hands (palms down, thumbs in) on the floor at shoulder width.
- Remaining in a tuck position (until your buttocks touch the mat), push off with the balls of your feet and roll backward, bending your elbows and bringing your hands, palms up, alongside your head. Your thumbs should be pointing toward your ears.

- As your buttocks then your shoulders touch the mat, untuck, push with your hands, and straighten your elbows to lift your body into a handstand.
- Keeping your knees straight, bend your hips to bring your feet down to the mat immediately.
- Bend your knees slightly to stand.

To Spot:

Pull child's ankles upward to handstand position. Then *quickly* slip your arm under her waist so she can bend over it for landing.

FORWARD TO BACKWARD ROLL

Purpose: Developing balance, coordination
Equipment: Mats or thick blankets (folded)
Play Area: Classroom (cleared), gym, or yard
Formation: Single-file lines facing mats (2 or 3) placed end-to-end.

Directions:

- With your legs crossed at the ankles, do a forward roll ending in a squat position.
- Remaining in a squat position, pivot to uncross your legs.
- Do a backward roll, ending in a standing position.

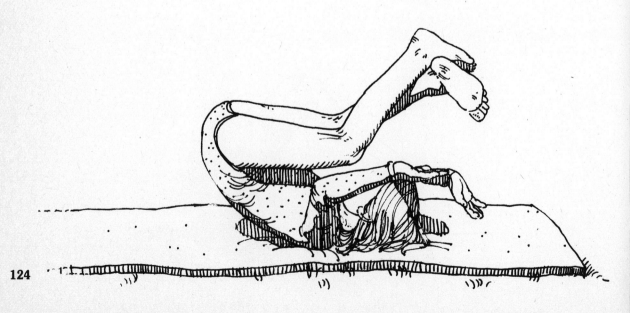

BALANCE BEAM ROUTINE

Purpose: Developing balance, coordination; learning to remember a movement sequence
Equipment: Low balance beam
Play Area: Classroom (cleared), gym, or yard
Formation: Single-file line facing one end of the balance beam.

Directions:

Set a routine or pattern and have each child do it, in turn, on the beam. You might start with

- Walk forward 4 steps. Squat and turn half way around. Walk forward (now in opposite direction) 4 steps. Walk off beam or dismount.
- Walk forward 4 steps. Hop forward 2 steps. Lower to a knee bend. Rise. Walk off beam or dismount.
- Walk forward 4 steps. Walk backward 4 steps. Do a quarter turn to one side. Do 4 crossover steps (left over right or right over left), moving sideways on the beam. Do another quarter turn. Walk off the beam or dismount.

Related Activities:

Arrange for children to attend a gymnastics meet at a nearby high school, college, or gymnastics center. Have them look for movements they know and note especially the way individual movements are combined to form routines.

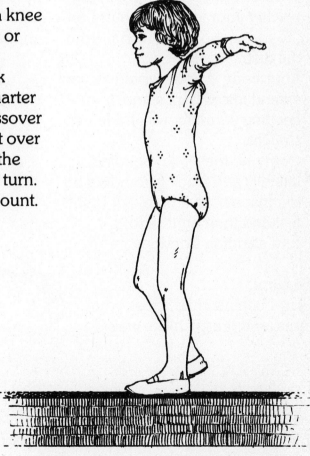

5

CARTWHEEL

Purpose: Developing strength, coordination
Equipment: Mats or thick blankets (folded)
Play Area: Classroom (cleared), gym, or yard
Formation: Single-file line facing mats (2 or 3) placed end-to-end. Be prepared to spot each child during his first few attempts to do this activity.

Directions:

- Stand with your side to the mat.
- Step onto the mat with your right (left) foot.
- Bending your right (left) knee slightly, place your right (left) hand on the mat in front of your foot.
- Thrust from your left (right) leg, placing your left (right) hand on the mat a shoulders' width from the first.
- Your body is now twisted as you extend into a handstand, keeping your elbows and knees straight.
- Continue the circle, bending laterally and placing your feet on the mat one at a time, left (right) first and then right (left).
- End standing sideways.

To Spot:

Stand behind child, cross your arms, and grasp child's waist.

Note:

This is a lifting not throwing stunt: the pelvis is lifted over the hands. It should be performed in a straight line. A straight line drawn or taped on the floor may help children learn proper hand and foot placement. The performer's eyes should be on the mat until he is ready to stand, ending the movement.

5

EVALUATION

Area: Stunts and Tumbling

Name _____ **Date of Observation** _____

Stunt	Check one or more
1. Backward Extension Roll	Assumes correct starting position ☐ Extends legs straight over hands ☐ Straightens arms completely ☐ Snaps to stand smoothly ☐
2. Balance Beam Routine	Smooth ☐ Maintains balance ☐ Performs complete routine ☐
3. Cartwheel	Places hands directly in front of legs ☐ Lifts pelvis over hands ☐ Reaches handstand position ☐ Bends laterally to stand ☐

Additional comments:

GAMES

6.

Games are an important part of any activity education program. They relieve tensions and encourage relaxation. They give each child an opportunity to learn new skills and to use and develop locomotor and nonlocomotor skills learned elsewhere. They allow children to experience what it means to be a team member. Ideally, they also offer all children a chance to participate.

Games in this chapter involve throwing, catching, dribbling, jumping, and running skills. Each game description specifies whether it should be played indoors or outdoors, in a yard, a classroom, or a gym.

The basic equipment needed for these games includes:
- balls
- a bottle (empty)
- dress-up clothes (2 sets) in paper bags or small suitcases
- newspaper, 2 two-page sheets for each team
- rope
- towel

Before teaching a new game, complete all preparations (drawing or establishing boundaries, rounding up equipment) and give children an opportunity to practice the locomotor skills involved. To keep children interested and alert throughout the game, give directions with enthusiasm and enforce rules with impartiality. After the children understand and have played the game several times, introduce a variation.

The lessons in this chapter are arranged from simple to complex. Many of the games near the end of the chapter include skills used in team sports. You may find it necessary to modify the tasks in each game to suit the ages and capabilities of the children playing. Demonstrations and/or chalkboard diagrams of the game may be useful in clarifying the directions.

6

DRESS-UP RELAY   20 MIN.

Purpose: Developing running skills, team spirit
Equipment: 2 paper bags or small suitcases, 2 sets of dress-up clothes
(*adult size* dress, suit coat and pants, hat, shoes, etc.)
Play Area: Classroom, gym
Formation: Divide the group into two teams. Have each team form a line behind the starting line.

Directions:

- Give each team a bag containing one set of clothes.
- Establish starting and turnaround points and a start signal.
- When the signal is given, one player from each team puts on the clothes in the bag, runs to turnaround point (or end of the room), takes off the clothes, puts them into the bag, and returns to the starting line where she hands the bag to the next person in line.
- Each member of the team repeats the procedure. The first team to finish wins.

Related Activities:

- Discuss clothing: What fabrics are used to make clothing? Where do these fabrics come from? How are they grown or produced? How are they processed (spun, dyed)? (E.g., you might talk about silk, cotton, wool, and synthetics.) How are they alike or different in the care that must be given them? How do you know? (Talk about labeling.)

6

- Talk about the history of clothing and fashion design. If possible, visit a museum to see how fashions have changed. Why have these changes taken place? If you could go back to any period in fashion history, what period would you choose?
- What special properties make certain items of clothing particularly useful or valuable? (E.g. flame retardancy, permanent press, etc.)
- Talk about clothing as a protection for the body. What fabric best protects against loss of body heat—even when wet? (Wool.) Why? (Because it dries from the inside out and thus maintains an insulating pocket of warm air between itself and the body.) What is *insulation*?
- Name some occupations, sports, or hobbies that require special clothing (e.g., wet suit for surfing or diving, leather suit for motocross racing, boots for horseback riding) and explain why the item you name is valuable.

- Talk about clothing as a costume, something that helps define the role being played. If possible, attend a play or watch one on television, paying particular attention to the costuming.
- Stage a skit based on the clothes used in the dress-up relay—and use some or all of them as costumes for those in the skit.
- How do the clothes you wear affect your mood? The way you see yourself? The role *you* play?

6

DODGE BALL   20-30 MIN.

Purpose: Developing throwing, dodging, catching skills
Equipment: Rubber ball
Play Area: Gym, yard
Formation: Two-thirds of the group form a large circle around the remaining players.

Directions:

- The players standing around the circle attempt to hit those inside the circle *below the waist* with the ball.
- When a player is hit, he changes places with the player who hit him.
- Repeat the game until all players have had a chance to dodge the ball.

- When the ball goes outside the circle, the closest player recovers it and brings it back to resume the game.

Variations:

- Use a different-shaped playing area.
- Use two balls.

ROCK, PAPER, SCISSORS   15 MIN.

Purpose: Indoor (rainy day) activity
Equipment: None
Play Area: Classroom, gym
Formation: Children choose partners and play in twos, or small groups can play, two at a time, with the "winner" playing the next person in the group.

Directions:

- Three hand motions are involved: two fingers V-shaped to show "scissors," a clenched fist for "rock," and an open hand for "paper."
- The players begin by saying, "One, two, three . . ." and then both extend one of their hands in one of the positions described above.
- The winner is determined when paper covers rock, rock breaks scissors, or scissors cut paper.

Related Activities:

- Talk about rocks: What does a *geologist* study? What is *lapidary*? What basic types of rocks are found in the world? (Igneous, metamorphic, and sedimentary.) How was each formed?
- Talk about paper: From what and how is it made? When and by whom was it first made? What is *papyrus*?
- Demonstrate and discuss the correct way to carry scissors and to hand them to someone.

6

NEWSPAPER RELAY   15-20 MIN.

Purpose: Developing team spirit, participation in a running activity
Equipment: 2 two-page sheets of newspaper per team
Play Area: Gym or yard
Formation: Divide the group into two or more teams. Establish a starting and a finish line. Have each team form a line behind the starting line.

Directions:

- Fold each newspaper sheet into quarters and give each team 2 folded sheets.
- To reach the finish line, each team member must put down one newspaper and step on it with one foot, then put down the other paper for the other foot, and so on until she reaches the finish line.
- Then she runs back to the starting line to give her newspapers to the next player in line.
- The first team finished wins.

Related Activities:

- Talk about newspapers: How are they written, printed, and distributed? Why, when it is possible to watch news broadcasts on television several times a day, are they still needed? How many trees must be grown and cut to meet current newsprint demands?
- Hold a paper drive to recycle some paper and save some of those trees.

- Look up and/or discuss:

journal	editorial
journalism	news story
yellow journalism	feature story
tabloid	font
responsible journalism	**boldface**
by-line	*italics*
dateline	roman
headline	sans serif
masthead	compositor
nameplate	editor
fact	reporter
opinion	proofreader

- If possible, visit a print shop.
- Plan, write, and publish at least one issue of a school, class, club, or group newspaper.

6

HANGMAN   20 MIN.

Purpose: Indoor (rainy day) activity
Equipment: Pencil and paper for each team
Play Area: Classroom
Formation: Divide group into twos or teams of two or more players.

Directions:

When played by two players,

- One of them thinks of a word or phrase and makes a dash for each letter in that word or phrase on a piece of paper, leaving extra space between words. He also draws a gallows on which to hang his man.
- The second player guesses a letter, and if it is one of the letters in the word, the first player writes it in the proper space. If the letter occurs more than once, he writes it in all spaces in which it should appear.
- If the guesser thinks of a letter that is not in the word, the first player draws a head on the hanging man. For the second wrong guess, he draws the body; the third, one arm; the fourth, the other arm; the fifth, one leg; the sixth, the other leg.

- The guesser tries to guess the right letters and fill in the blanks before the entire hanging man is drawn.

When played by teams, the game is the same except that the team members take turns guessing the letters, and the first one to complete the word wins for his team.

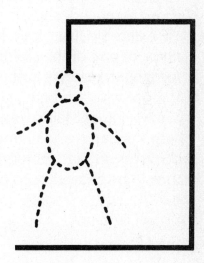

6

135

STREETS AND ALLEYS   20 MIN.

Purpose: Developing running and dodging skills
Equipment: None
Play Area: Gym or yard
Formation: Children stand in three or more equal rows with their arms outstretched so that each child touches fingertips with the child on either side. One child is "it" and must chase two other children through the "streets" and "alleys" thus formed.

Directions:

- When the leader says "streets," all remain in starting position.
- When the leader says "alleys," all turn one quarter turn to the right.
- "It" chases two other players through these streets and alleys. If one is tagged, she becomes "it," and the first "it" takes the place of one of the children forming the streets and alleys.
- If those who are being chased are not caught fairly frequently, stop the game and change positions so that everyone has a turn to be chased or to be "it."

Note:

- The game will be more exciting if the leader watches the chase closely and frequently calls for a change from streets to alleys and back to streets.
- Neither "it" nor those she is chasing are allowed to break through the outstretched arms of players.

FOUR SQUARE   20-30 MIN.

Purpose: Developing ball handling skills
Equipment: Four square court drawn, painted, or taped; rubber ball or volleyball for each group. The court is a large square divided into quarters with each quarter measuring 5 to 8 feet on a side.
Play Area: Yard
Formation: Four players, one in each square, with others waiting for a turn.

Directions:

- Serve begins from square 1. To serve, the child in square 1 drops the ball and serves underhand after the ball bounces.
- The server hits the ball to any of the other three players.
- The player who receives the ball must let it bounce once in his square, then hit it to another square.
- The player who receives it next keeps the ball in play in the same manner, letting it bounce once in his square, then hitting it to another player.
- Play continues until one of the following faults occurs:
  1. The ball is hit overhand.
  2. The ball lands on a line between the squares (ball on outside line is considered "good").
  3. One player steps in another player's square to hit the ball.
  4. One player catches or holds the ball before returning it.
  5. One player hits the ball with some part of his body other than his hand.
- When a fault is committed, the player who was in error goes to the end of the waiting line, all players move up (player in square 2 moves to square 1, player in square 3 moves to square 2, player in square 4 moves to square 3), and the new player starts in square 4.

BOX BALL   20-25 MIN.

Purpose: Developing running and throwing skills
Equipment: A box and ball for each team
Play Area: Yard, gym
Formation: Four teams, each with the same number of players (6 to 10). Each team stands on one side of a square. Boxes are placed in the center of the square. Each team member is given a number.

Directions:

- When a number is called, each child with that number runs to his team's box, picks up the ball, runs back to the head of his line, and gives the ball to the first person in line, who passes it to the next person and on down the line.
- When the ball reaches the last person on the team, he returns it to the box. The first team to return the ball scores a point.

- The runner need not resume his original position after he has carried the ball, but all children must remember their numbers to avoid confusion and players must adjust their spacing so that everyone has room to stand comfortably.

Note:
Be sure each child gets a turn to be runner.

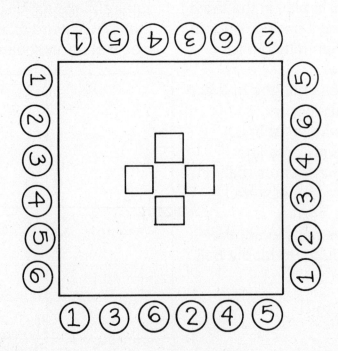

6

CHAIN TAG   20-30 MIN.

Purpose: Developing running and dodging skills
Equipment: None
Play Area: Yard or gym with playing area clearly established.
Formation: Well spaced with one player chosen to be "it" and tag other players.

Directions:

- "It" runs after and tries to catch the other players, who must remain within the established playing area.
- When a player is tagged, she joins hands with "it" to form a chain, and *together* they chase other players.
- Each additional player caught joins the chain.
- Only players at each end can tag others.
- If the chain breaks, tagging stops until the chain is reformed.
- For a large group, more than one chain may be started.
- Continue playing until all are caught or time is up.

CROWN THE KING   20-30 MIN.

Purpose: Developing ball handling and blocking skills
Equipment: Chair and ball
Play Area: Yard or gym
Formation: The "king" sits on a chair inside a circle 15 or more feet in diameter while another player acts as guard and tries to protect the king. All the other players remain outside the circle.

Directions:

- Players outside the circle take turns throwing the ball and trying to hit ("crown") the king *below the waist*.

- When a player crowns the king, he takes the place of the guard and the guard becomes the new king. The old king joins the other players outside the circle.

- The guard tries to keep the king from being hit with the ball. He can block the ball with his feet or legs, but cannot kick the ball. He can catch the ball to keep it from hitting or crowning the king, and then he returns it to the players outside the circle.

Related Activities:

- Talk about kings: Are some countries still ruled by kings? Which ones? Why might a king need a guard?

- Does the President of the United States have a guard? Why?

- Look up and/or discuss:

caesar	pharaoh
czar	potentate
dictator	ruler
emperor	tyrant
king	

6

JUMP THE SHOT   10-25 MIN.

Purpose: Developing jumping skills
Equipment: 20-foot rope with a knotted towel tied to one end
Play Area: Yard or gym
Formation: Single circle facing the oncoming rope and towel; one player stands in the center holding the rope with the knotted towel tied to one end.

Directions:
- Keeping the towel near the floor or ground, the player in the center swings the rope in a large circle.
- As the towel comes close to those players standing in the circle, they jump to avoid being hit by it. They must not step out of the circle.
- If the rope touches a player's feet, he is "out."
- The last remaining player becomes the new rope turner.

Note:
- The rope must be kept low.
- Speed of the turns can be increased and decreased.
- Select a new center player every few minutes.

BALL AND STICK RELAY   20-30 MIN.

Purpose: Developing ball handling skills and team spirit
Equipment: A ball and wand or stick for each team
Play Area: Yard, gym
Formation: Establish a starting and midway line. Divide the group into relay teams. Have each team form a line behind the starting line.

Directions:
- In turn, each player pushes the ball with the stick up to the midway point and then back across the starting line to the next player on her team.
- The first team to finish wins.

Variations:
Carry the ball to the midway point, then push it back across the line with the stick. Reverse this procedure.

6

TEAM DODGE BALL   20 MIN.

Purpose: Developing ball handling and dodging skills
Equipment: Ball
Play Area: Yard, gym
Formation: Divide players into two teams. Members of one team stand inside a circle formed by members of the other team.

Directions:

- Players forming the circle throw the ball at players inside the circle, attempting to hit them below the waist.
- As a player is hit, he moves away from the circle and sits down.
- After two minutes, the players who are out are counted and the teams change positions.
- The team with the most players out after each has had a turn loses; the team who put the most players out is the winner.
- Once a player is out, he stays out until the teams change places.

6

FIND A PLACE   20 MIN.

Purpose: Indoor (rainy day) activity
Equipment: None
Play Area: Gym, classroom
Formation: Players stand in a circle around "it." All players are given a number; several have each number given.

Directions:
- "It" calls any two numbers.
- Players having those numbers try to exchange places.
- "It" tries to take one of the resulting open places in the circle.
- Whoever is left without a place is "it" for the next time and must call two new numbers.

Note:
Be sure "it" remains in the center of the circle until she has called both numbers!

144

HINDU TAG   20 MIN.

Purpose: Developing running skills
Equipment: None
Play Area: Gym, yard (if grassy)
Formation: Free formation inside a limited playing area; one player is
"it." Separate boys and girls into two groups.

Directions:

- The player who is "it" tries to tag another player.
- A player is safe when she assumes the Hindu position, that is, when she kneels, puts her hands on the floor or ground, palms down, and rests her forehead on the backs of her hands.

Note:

Practice the Hindu position before the game is begun.

6

145

KEEP AWAY   20 MIN.

Purpose: Developing ball handling skills and team spirit
Equipment: Ball; colored bands, shirts, uniform, etc. to distinguish
teams
Play Area: Yard, gym
Formation: Two teams scattered over the play area.

Directions:

- Establish stopping and starting signal (whistle).
- Toss the ball into the play area.
- Players attempt to control the ball and pass it among their own team members while the opponents try to recover the ball.

- If two opponents catch a pass at the same time, the leader tosses the ball up between the two players; each attempts to hit the ball to his own team.
- No points are scored: the game is played for fun.

RESCUE RELAY   15-20 MIN.

Purpose: Developing running skills
Equipment: None
Play Area: Gym, yard
Formation: Two teams in relay formation behind starting line. One player from each team stands on the goal line and faces his team.

Directions:

- When the signal is given, the player on the goal line runs to his team, takes a hand of the first player in line, and runs with him back to the goal line.

- The player just brought to the goal line repeats this procedure with the next player in line.
- Each player continues until all are "rescued" and are in relay formation on the goal line.

6

TEAM SPORTS

7.

Traditional team sports should seldom be taught in their entirety. Doing so causes children to waste time *trying* to play a game before they have mastered the skills that are fundamental to it. Instead, time and care should first be given to improving basic movement patterns, because success in playing such team sports as soccer, tag football, volleyball, basketball, and softball depends on the ability to execute correctly varying combinations of these patterns.

Because basic rule books for team sports are available in most sporting goods stores, this chapter is devoted to helping you recognize and develop in your children those fundamentals essential for success in these sports. It takes considerable practice to develop physical fitness and efficient locomotion, to throw with speed and accuracy, to catch accurately, to hit and strike with consistency, to maintain balance, and to become skilled in strategic movements. To make skill practice fun, various parts of a team sport may be played as ''lead-up'' games. Break down the sports into playable parts, practice these parts individually until they can be performed with a high degree of success, then play the whole game.

7

SOCCER

Fundamental Skills: The fundamental skills needed to play soccer successfully are kicking, blocking, and dribbling.

Kicking

Soccer is basically a game played with the feet. To play it well, a child must develop sufficient balance and locomotor skills to permit him to move quickly over a field in pursuit, stop abruptly, and balance on one leg while swinging the other to kick the ball. Timing, balance, approaching the ball from a slight angle, and developing a good leg swing are the secrets of soccer kicking.

Children should practice kicking a stationary, rolling, and then bounding ball for both distance and accuracy. For most kicking, they should use the instep, that part of the foot covered by the laces of the shoe: the toe is less accurate.

To practice the kick,
- Place the nonkicking foot alongside the ball.
- Keep your head down, your eyes on the ball.
- Maintain good balance, extending your arms as needed.
- As your kicking foot makes contact with the ball, bend the knee of your kicking leg slightly.
- After making contact with the ball, allow your kicking leg to complete its forward motion (this is called the follow-through), ending with the toe pointed downward.

Instep kick.

Blocking

There are three major kinds of blocks. These are termed

1) BODY BLOCK, in which a player sags slightly backward as the ball hits his body to prevent it from ricocheting wildly;

2) HEADING, in which a player passes, scores, clears, or controls the ball by hitting it with his forehead just below the hairline; and

3) TRAPPING, in which a player stops the oncoming ball with the inside or outside of his foot or the sole of his shoe.

Body block.

Sole-of-foot trap.

Heading.

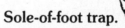

Inside foot trap.

7

151

Dribbling

In soccer dribbling is one means of moving the ball forward. It involves advancing the ball, under control, by giving it short kicks or pushes with the inside or outside of the foot while outmaneuvering an opponent in his efforts to gain control of it.

Dribbling.

Skill Drills

The following drills may be used to improve the basic skills of kicking, blocking, and dribbling:

- dribble and pass relay,
- partner's relay,
- dribble relay,
- circle soccer pass,
- zigzag kick,
- soccer goal kick, and
- kicking, blocking, and dribbling for accuracy.

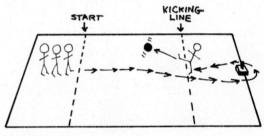

Dribble and pass relay.

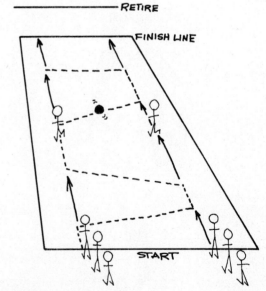

Partner's relay.

7

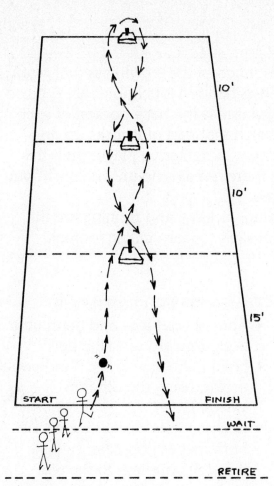

Dribble relay.

Circle soccer pass.

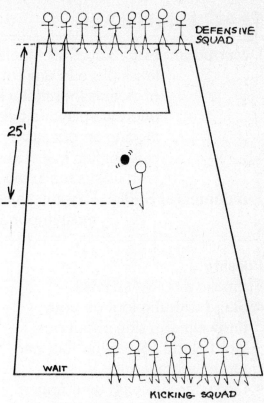

Soccer goal kick.

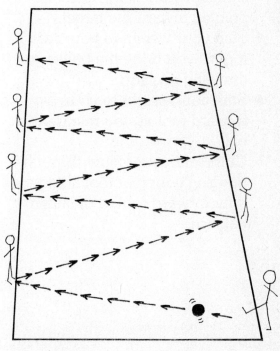

Zigzag kick.

FLAG FOOTBALL

Description: Flag football eliminates much of the roughness that often takes place in one- or two-handed touch football. A piece of cloth is loosely tucked under the back portion of each offensive player's belt such that part of it sticks up. In tagging an offensive player, a defensive player pulls this cloth or flag free. Thus there remains no uncertainty about who was actually tagged.

Fundamental Skills: Passing, catching, kicking, and running are the most important skills to learn in flag football.

Passing

To make a FORWARD PASS,

- Stand with the foot on your throwing arm side about one foot behind your other foot and turned slightly out.
- Grasp the ball with your fingers spread around its rear portion.
- Hold the ball above your shoulder with its forward end pointed toward the target.
- Shift your weight to your rear foot as you bring the ball to a throwing position.
- Shift your weight to your forward foot as you release the ball.
- Complete your follow-through, bringing your rear foot alongside your forward foot to maintain balance.

To execute the CENTER PASS,

- Spread your legs and bend your body forward over the ball.
- Hold the ball with the hand you prefer, using the other to steady it.
- Balance your weight evenly on both feet as you pass the ball through your legs to the rear and up.

Passing.

7

Receiving

To receive a FORWARD PASS,

- Keep your eyes on the ball and maneuver to put yourself in position to receive it.
- Hold your hands open and relaxed with palms turned upward.
- After you have caught the ball, tighten your grip on it and draw it in close to your body.

To receive a PUNT,

- Keep your eyes on the oncoming ball.
- Extend your hands to meet it, keeping them open and relaxed.
- As the catch is made, bring the ball in close to your body.

Receiving.

155

7

Kicking

To PUNT,

- Hold the ball (laces up, parallel to the ground) with both hands, placing your left hand on the left front side of the ball, your right hand on the right rear.
- Carrying the ball with you, step forward on your right foot, take a long step with your left foot, and then kick with your right.
- Release the ball over your right foot as you make contact with your right instep.
- After the kick, bring your right foot back and down immediately to maintain your balance.

The PLACE KICK is made with the toe slightly below the ball center line.

Running

Successful running in football requires

- a quick start,
- the ability to change pace,
- good balance,
- deceptive change of direction, and
- powerful leg muscles.

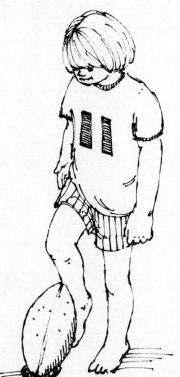

7

156 **Kicking.**

Skill Drills

The following drills may be used to improve basic skills needed in football:

- center and forward pass relay,
- punt practice,
- serpentine relay, and
- pass practice.

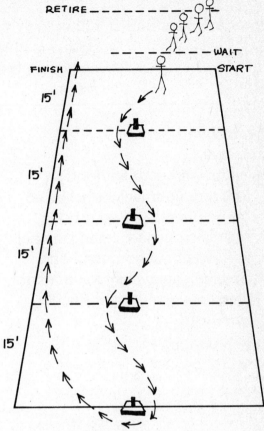

Serpentine relay.

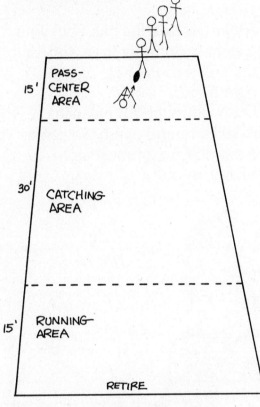

Center and forward pass relay.

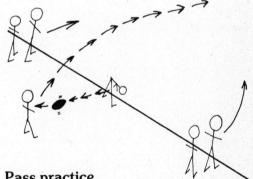

Pass practice.

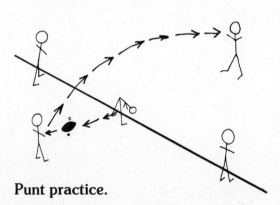

Punt practice.

VOLLEYBALL

Fundamental Skills: Other than strategy and teamwork, the primary skills one must master to be a successful volleyball player are the underhand serve and the volleyball return.

Underhand Serve

To serve,

- Stand with your left foot forward, your weight balanced on both feet, and your body slightly crouched, resting the ball in the palm of your left hand.
- Shifting your weight to your right foot, move your right hand backward.

- As you release the ball, shift your weight to your left foot, and hit the ball with the heel of your right hand.
- Follow through for balance.

The sidearm and overhead serves are too difficult for most eight- to twelve-year-olds.

Underhand serve.

7

Volleyball Returns

To execute the underhand volley, the overhand volley, and to set up the ball,

- Keep your eyes on the ball.
- Use both hands.
- Try to maintain good balance.
- Avoid touching the ball with the palms of your hands: use your fingers instead.

Underhand volley.   Overhand volley.   159

Skill Drills
The following drills may be used to improve basic skills needed in volleyball:

- serve,
- volley relay,
- serve relay,
- return, and
- set-up.

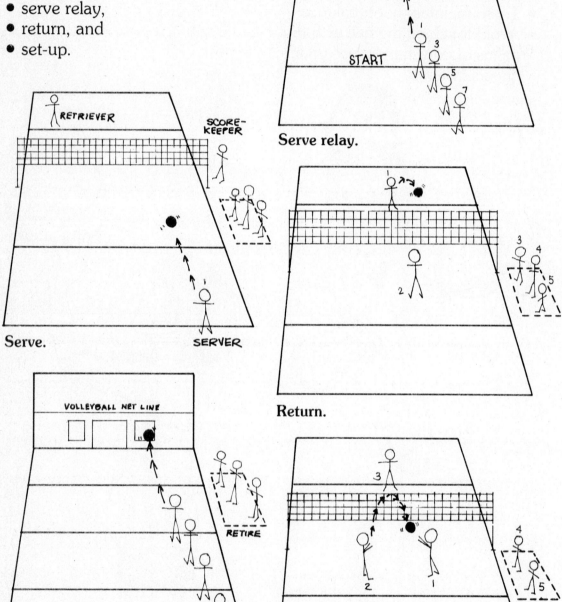

Serve relay.

Serve.

Return.

Volley relay.

Set-up.

160

VOLLEYBALL SCORE SHEET

Date_____ Court _____ Time_____

TEAM _____

LF	
CF	
RF	
LB	
CB	
RB	

TEAM _____

LF	
CF	
RF	
LB	
CB	
RB	

GAME I

1 2 3 4 5 6 7 8 9 10 11 12 13 14 15 16 17 18 19 20 21	Score

GAME I

1 2 3 4 5 6 7 8 9 10 11 12 13 14 15 16 17 18 19 20 21	Score

GAME II

1 2 3 4 5 6 7 8 9 10 11 12 13 14 15 16 17 18 19 20 21	Score

GAME II

1 2 3 4 5 6 7 8 9 10 11 12 13 14 15 16 17 18 19 20 21	Score

GAME III

1 2 3 4 5 6 7 8 9 10 11 12 13 14 15 16 17 18 19 20 21	Score

GAME III

1 2 3 4 5 6 7 8 9 10 11 12 13 14 15 16 17 18 19 20 21	Score

Winner_____ Referee _____

BASKETBALL

Fundamental Skills: The fundamental skills needed in basketball are catching, passing, dribbling, and shooting.

Catching

To catch,

- Keep your eyes on the ball.
- Extend your arms. If the catch is to be made above the waist, keep your thumbs together; if it is to be made below the waist, keep your little fingers together.

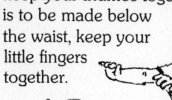

Passing

The underhand, overhand, chest, overhead, and shoulder passes are the ones used most often by children between the ages of eight and twelve. Whenever possible they should use both hands in passing the ball because their hands are usually not large enough to make controlled one-hand passes. Teach them to lead the running receiver with their bounce and air passes.

Chest pass.

162 Overhead pass.

Shoulder pass.

Dribbling

In basketball a player must dribble or bounce the ball as he moves with it. The ball should be pushed with the fingers, never slapped or batted. It should never bounce higher than the dribbler's waist and is less likely to be stolen by an opponent if dribbled only knee high.

Shooting

Children of this age should concentrate on the chest, one-hand, and two-hand set shots and the lay-up. In most instances they will be unable to control jump and hook shots.

One-hand set shot.

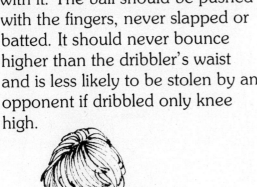

Dribbling.

Lay-up shot.

Skill Drills

The following drills may be used to improve basic skills needed in basketball:

- dribble, pivot, and pass relay, and
- serpentine dribble relay.

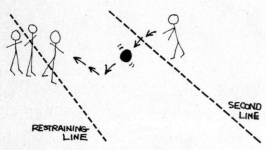

Dribble, pivot, and pass relay.

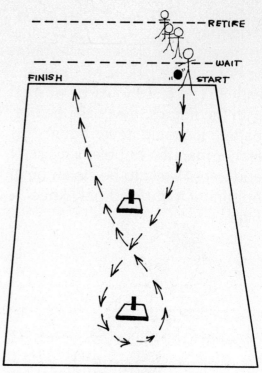

Serpentine dribble relay.

BASKETBALL SCORE SHEET

League _____ Gym _____ Date _____

TEAM _____

Name	Number	Summary			
		Fouls	Field Goals	Free Throws	Total Points
F					
F					
F					
F					
C					
C					
G					
G					
G					
G					
Team Totals					

Time Outs: 1 2 3 4 5

Running Score: 1   2   3   4   5   6   7   8   9   10   11   12   13   14   15   16   17   18   19   20   21   22
23 24 25 26 27 28 29 30 31 32 33 34 35 36 37 38 39 40 41 42 43 44 45 46 47 48 49 50

TEAM _____

Name	Number	Summary			
		Fouls	Field Goals	Free Throws	Total Points
F					
F					
F					
F					
C					
C					
G					
G					
G					
G					
Team Totals					

Time Outs: 1 2 3 4 5

Running Score: 1   2   3   4   5   6   7   8   9   10   11   12   13   14   15   16   17   18   19   20   21   22
23 24 25 26 27 28 29 30 31 32 33 34 35 36 37 38 39 40 41 42 43 44 45 46 47 48 49 50

Referee _____ Umpire _____

Scorer _____ Round _____ Attendance _____

SOFTBALL

Fundamental Skills: Essential to softball are the skills associated with throwing, catching, and batting.

Throwing

All children should be taught how to throw both overhand and underhand. Teach them to use their body, not just their arms, when throwing and to throw accurately.

Throwing (overhand).

Pitching.

7

Catching

To catch,

- Keep your eyes on the ball.
- Extend your arms and relax your hands.
- Allow your hands and arms to give with the impact of the ball.

- In catches made below the waist, your little fingers should be close to one another. In catching above your waist, place your thumbs close to one another.

Catching a ground ball.

Catching a fly ball.

167

Batting
To bat,
- Stand with your right (left) foot about 12 to 18 inches behind your left (right) foot and turned slightly out.
- Grip the bat with both hands, right (left) above left (right) and hold it over your right (left) shoulder.
- Keep your eyes on the ball.
- As it approaches, swing your bat forward and slightly down, twisting your body and shifting your weight at the moment of impact to your left (right) foot.
- Follow through, bringing the bat on around after impact and bringing your right (left) foot forward.

Using a batting tee may help a child correct her swing.

Skill Drills
The following drills may be used to improve basic skills needed in softball:
- tee-ball,
- double play,
- relays, and
- base running.

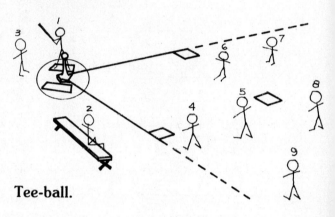

Tee-ball.

168   **Batting.**

SOFTBALL SCORE SHEET

League _____ Field _____ Date _____

Time _____ Officials _____

TEAM _____

Name	Position	Innings								
		1	2	3	4	5	6	7	8	9

TEAM _____

Name	Position	Innings								
		1	2	3	4	5	6	7	8	9

SUMMARY OF SCORING BY INNINGS

Teams	1	2	3	4	5	6	7	8	9	Total

SCORING SYMBOLS: S, Single; **D**, Double; **T**, Triple; **HR**, Home Run; **K**, Strikeout; **SB**, Stolen Base; **B**, Base on Balls; **H**, Hit by Pitch; **W**, Wild Pitch; **P**, Passed Ball; **Bk**, Balk Run; **FC**, Fielder's Choice; **E**, Error.
POSITION NUMBERS:1, Pitcher; **2**, Catcher; **3**, First Base; **4**, Second Base; **5**, Third Base; **6**, Short Stop; **7**, Left Field; **8**, Center Field; **9**, Right Field.

TOURNAMENTS

Tournaments can be used as effectively with skill drills as when playing the full game. You might want to keep in mind such types of tournaments as the ladder, the pyramid, the elimination, the elimination-consolation, and the round robin when organizing your practice sessions.

Ladder Tournament

The ladder tournament is best used for conducting competition that may be played off informally by contestants when they choose and may last as long as desired. For example, if you hold such a tournament for basketball free throws (most free throws completed in twenty-five tries), you arrange the players' names on the ladder with the most skilled at the bottom. A child can move up the ladder by challenging either of the two persons whose names appear immediately above his own. If his challenge is successful and he wins, he changes positions on the ladder with the person he challenged and beat. You may wish to set a minimum number of challenges and acceptances to be held each week.

This kind of tournament is appropriate for a large number of specific drills and games, such as sprints, the high jump, throwing for accuracy, and table tennis.

Pyramid Tournaments

The principles of the pyramid tournament are the same as those of the ladder tournament except that each child is allowed to challenge the child whose name appears in the block to the left of, or immediately above, his own.

Elimination Tournament

The elimination tournament is the easiest to conduct. It may be used in skill drills or in the playing of various games. Those children who seem most skilled are seeded so they will not meet one another until the final stages of the tournament. If there are not enough players or teams to fill all slots, a bye may be used.

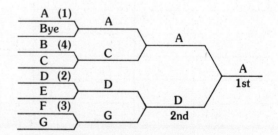

Correct organization of an elimination tournament when the number of teams is not a perfect power of two. The number in parentheses indicates the order in which players are seeded.

Elimination-Consolation

This type of tournament prevents the first-round losers from being completely out of the tournament. Instead, they play other first-round losers to determine a consolation winner.

Round Robin

In this type of tournament, participation is at a maximum. Every player or team plays every other player or team. Tournament organization for a league having four, five, six, seven, eight, or nine teams is shown on page 175.

Elimination-consolation tournament.

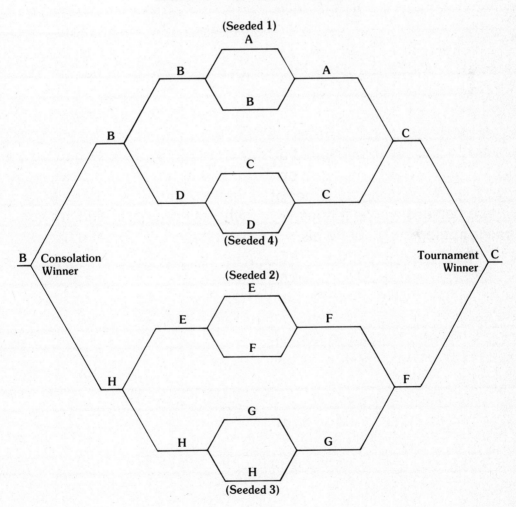

171

LADDER TOURNAMENT

1

2

3

4

5

6

7

8

9

10

11

12

PYRAMID TOURNAMENT

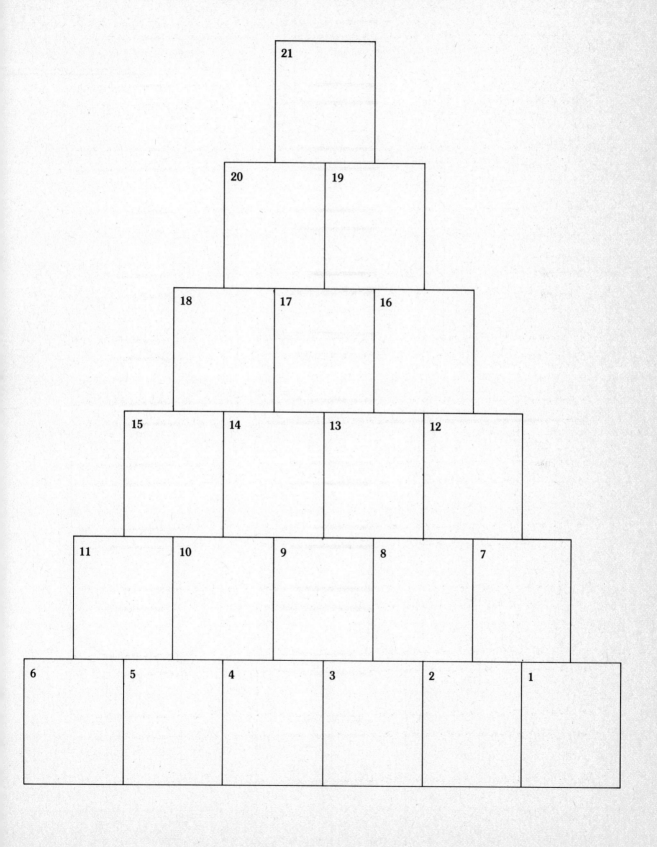

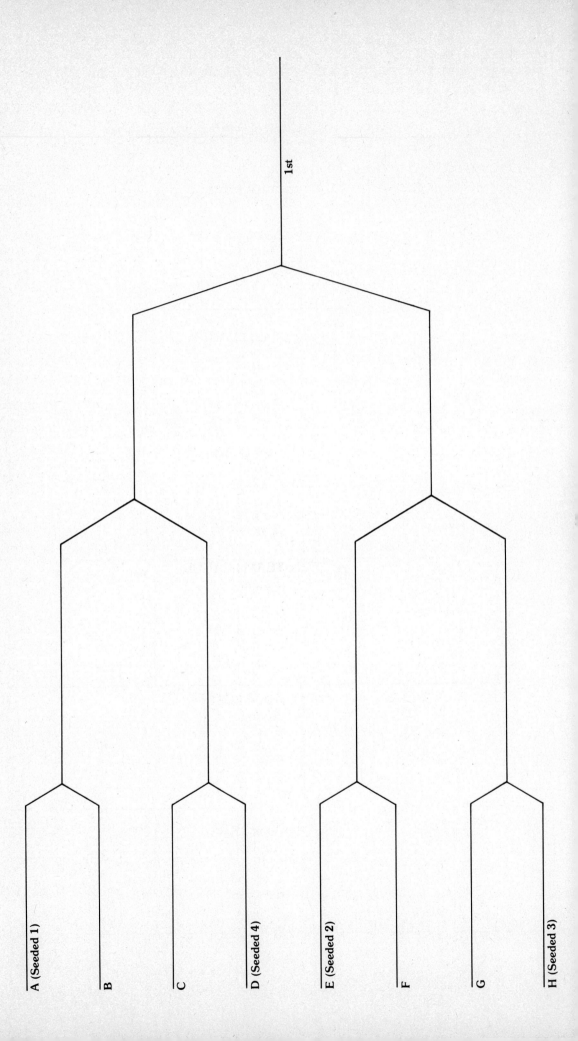

ELIMINATION TOURNAMENT

1st

A (Seeded 1)

B

C

D (Seeded 4)

E (Seeded 2)

F

G

H (Seeded 3)

ROUND ROBIN TOURNAMENT

Directions:

Substitute the name of each team for a number and follow through with each round of play.

FOUR-TEAM LEAGUE
Round

I	II	III
1 vs. 2	1 vs. 3	1 vs. 4
3 vs. 4	2 vs. 4	2 vs. 3

FIVE-TEAM LEAGUE
Round

I	II	III	IV	V
1 vs. X	1 vs. 2	1 vs. 3	1 vs. 4	1 vs. 5
2 vs. 5	3 vs. X	4 vs. 2	5 vs. 3	X vs. 4
3 vs. 4	4 vs. 5	5 vs. X	X vs. 2	2 vs. 3

SIX-TEAM LEAGUE
Round

I	II	III	IV	V
1 vs. 6	1 vs. 2	1 vs. 3	1 vs. 4	1 vs. 5
2 vs. 5	3 vs. 6	4 vs. 2	5 vs. 3	6 vs. 4
3 vs. 4	4 vs. 5	5 vs. 6	6 vs. 2	2 vs. 3

SEVEN-TEAM LEAGUE
Round

I	II	III	IV	V	VI	VII
1 vs. X	1 vs. 2	1 vs. 3	1 vs. 4	1 vs. 5	1 vs. 6	1 vs. 7
2 vs. 7	3 vs. X	4 vs. 2	5 vs. 3	6 vs. 4	7 vs. 5	X vs. 6
3 vs. 6	4 vs. 7	5 vs. X	6 vs. 2	7 vs. 3	X vs. 4	2 vs. 5
4 vs. 5	5 vs. 6	6 vs. 7	7 vs. X	X vs. 2	2 vs. 3	3 vs. 4

EIGHT-TEAM LEAGUE
Round

I	II	III	IV	V	VI	VII
1 vs. 8	1 vs. 2	1 vs. 3	1 vs. 4	1 vs. 5	1 vs. 6	1 vs. 7
2 vs. 7	3 vs. 8	4 vs. 2	5 vs. 3	6 vs. 4	7 vs. 5	8 vs. 6
3 vs. 6	4 vs. 7	5 vs. 8	6 vs. 2	7 vs. 3	8 vs. 4	2 vs. 5
4 vs. 5	5 vs. 6	6 vs. 7	7 vs. 8	8 vs. 2	2 vs. 3	3 vs. 4

NINE-TEAM LEAGUE
Round

I	II	III	IV	V	VI	VII	VIII	IX
1 vs. X	1 vs. 2	1 vs. 3	1 vs. 4	1 vs. 5	1 vs. 6	1 vs. 7	1 vs. 8	1 vs. 9
2 vs. 9	3 vs. X	5 vs. 2	5 vs. 3	6 vs. 4	7 vs. 5	8 vs. 6	9 vs. 7	X vs. 8
3 vs. 8	4 vs. 9	6 vs. X	6 vs. 2	7 vs. 3	8 vs. 4	9 vs. 5	X vs. 6	2 vs. 7
4 vs. 7	5 vs. 8	7 vs. 9	7 vs. X	8 vs. 2	9 vs. 3	X vs. 4	2 vs. 5	3 vs. 6
5 vs. 6	6 vs. 7	8 vs. 8	8 vs. 9	9 vs. X	X vs. 2	2 vs. 3	3 vs. 4	4 vs. 5

FORMS

Forms of many kinds are often used by leaders of activity education programs. Several examples of such forms have been included here. They are a track and field master score sheet, a percentage table, an injury report form, and two evaluation forms.

The score sheet is self-explanatory. The percentage table is designed to help players or teams keep records of their winning or losing percentages. The injury report form gives you a standardized method for keeping track of injuries and their causes and disposition. The evaluation forms may be used to stimulate children to become more effective in leadership roles. These forms can be reproduced for use as is or can serve as samples for forms you tailor to meet your own needs.

7

TRACK AND FIELD MASTER SCORE SHEET

Organization	60-Yard Dash	70-Yard High Hurdles	¾-Mile Run	100-Yard Dash	70-Yard Low Hurdles	300-Yard Run	High Jump	Broad Jump	Shot Put	440-Yard Relay	Pole Vault	Discus Throw	880-Yard Relay	Total

Note:
The usual method for scoring track and field events in which several teams or organizations compete is to assign individual performance points in each event as follows:

First place—5 points
Second place—3 points
Third place—2 points
Fourth place—1 point

Team or organization scores can then be computed by adding up the individual performance scores of all members.

PERCENTAGE TABLE

		Games Won													
Games Lost	**1**	**2**	**3**	**4**	**5**	**6**	**7**	**8**	**9**	**10**	**11**	**12**	**13**	**14**	**15**
1	.500	.667	.750	.800	.833	.857	.875	.889	.900	.909	.917	.923	.929	.933	.938
2	.333	.500	.600	.667	.714	.750	.778	.800	.818	.833	.846	.857	.867	.875	.882
3	.250	.400	.500	.571	.625	.667	.700	.727	.750	.769	.786	.800	.813	.824	.833
4	.200	.333	.428	.500	.556	.600	.636	.667	.692	.714	.733	.750	.764	.778	.789
5	.167	.286	.375	.444	.500	.545	.583	.615	.643	.667	.688	.706	.722	.737	.750
6	.143	.250	.333	.400	.455	.500	.538	.571	.600	.625	.647	.667	.684	.700	.714
7	.125	.222	.300	.364	.417	.462	.500	.533	.563	.588	.611	.633	.650	.667	.682
8	.111	.200	.273	.333	.385	.428	.467	.500	.529	.556	.579	.600	.619	.636	.652
9	.100	.182	.250	.308	.357	.400	.438	.471	.500	.526	.550	.571	.591	.609	.625
10	.091	.167	.231	.286	.333	.375	.412	.444	.474	.500	.524	.545	.565	.583	.600
11	.083	.154	.214	.267	.313	.353	.389	.421	.450	.476	.500	.522	.542	.560	.576
12	.077	.143	.200	.250	.294	.333	.368	.400	.428	.455	.478	.500	.520	.538	.556
13	.071	.133	.188	.235	.278	.316	.350	.381	.408	.435	.458	.480	.500	.519	.536
14	.067	.125	.176	.222	.263	.300	.338	.364	.391	.417	.400	.462	.481	.500	.517
15	.063	.118	.167	.211	.250	.286	.318	.348	.375	.400	.423	.444	.464	.483	.500

INJURY REPORT

Name of person injured _____ Phone _____

Address _____ Date _____

Activity _____ Time _____

Place where accident occurred _____

Cause and nature of injury _____

_____

_____

Type of first aid given _____

_____

_____

Disposition _____

_____

_____

WITNESSES

_____   _____

_____   _____

CAUSE OF ACCIDENT

☐ Poor equipment   ☐ Poor playing surface

☐ Bad judgment, carelessness   ☐ Poor illumination

☐ Lack of skill   ☐ Inadequate space

Other (describe) _____

_____

Person in charge _____   Person making report _____

LEADERSHIP EVALUATION

NAME _____ DATE _____

CRITIC/OBSERVER _____

1. PERSONAL IMPRESSION	HIGH TO LOW				
	5	4	3	2	1
Dress					
Voice					
Posture					
Grooming					
Poise before the group					
Freedom from mannerisms					

2. ATTITUDE	5	4	3	2	1
Attendance					
Promptness					
Initiative					
Responses					
Enthusiasm					
Adjustment					
Resourcefulness					
Confidence					
Willingness to take criticism					
Professional characteristics					

3. ABILITY	5	4	3	2	1
To control the group					
To plan					
To organize					
To follow through					
To evidence knowledge of activity					
To recognize individual differences					
To arouse interest					
To use language appropriately					

4. PREDICTION	5	4	3	2	1
Future expectations for the leader					

REMARKS: _____

_____

LEADER'S SELF-EVALUATION CHECKLIST

	HIGH TO LOW				
	5	4	3	2	1
1. Have I considered the needs of all members?					
2. Have I provided an adequate number and variety of activities?					
3. Have I divided the group adequately for maximum participation?					
4. Does my program allow for maximum skill development?					
5. Have I sufficiently helped those who need help most?					
6. Have I curtailed the movements of the overactive?					
7. Have I introduced new activities with enthusiasm?					
8. Have I fostered the development of cooperative attitudes?					
9. Did the participants have fun?					
10. Were the experiences participated in worthwhile?					
11. Did the experiences contribute to character development?					
12. Was there evidence in the participants of physical, mental, and social growth?					

Score of:

55-60	Excellent
48-54	Good
40-47	Average
34-39	Fair
38 or less	Poor

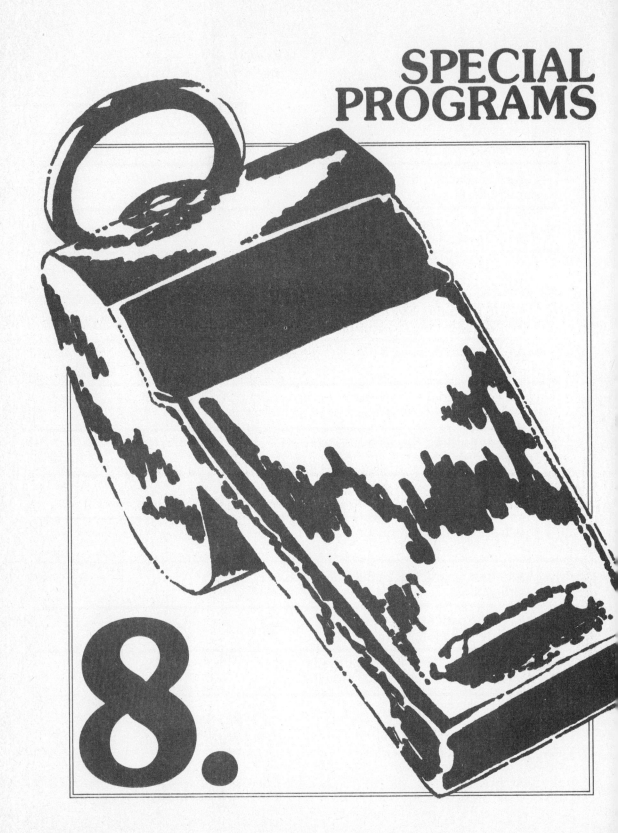

SPECIAL PROGRAMS

8.

You may wish to include in your recreation or activity education program some special programs, such as nature study, camping, or crafts. Depending on your approach and the specific needs of your group, such programs may give children a chance to learn new skills, to apply skills previously learned in a new setting, or to create and to appreciate what they and others have created. They may be a welcome change of pace and a ready reply to, "I'm bored. I don't have anything to do." And some are suitable for inclement weather.

NATURE STUDY

For most people, nature is readily at hand but often missed or dismissed amid life's rush. Yet many find real recreation in "getting back" to it, in discovering and experiencing some of its elemental rhythms.

In many areas such an experience may be as close as the open doorway: you need only walk through and then stand still—or sit—and smell, feel, listen, and watch. Sometimes, however, it is difficult to see what you look at all the time, and nature's wonders are more apparent in a new and different setting, such as a

- beach
- bird sanctuary
- creek
- field
- forest
- public garden
- museum
- park
- pond
- tide pool
- zoo

Many such places have guides who can help you and your group interpret your observations.

Unless you have acquired some expertise in identifying and describing indigenous flora and fauna, you may feel more qualified to lead a nature get-acquainted session rather than a nature study. All you need do is help the children learn to look, to *see*, to think about, to ask about, and to compare. You might

- Watch and make drawings to show how a particular tree changes with the seasons.

- Observe and indicate on a prepared horizon line where the sun seems to go down each Monday and at what time. Try to make your observations from the same place each time.
- Lay a length of string around an area of ground and then see what natural activity you can observe within its borders.
- Grow and care for any kind of plants, indoors or out.

You might like to take a nature walk or hike. If so, describe to the children the terrain they will cover and what particular features they should look for.

- Will they see many **trees**? What kinds? Maybe someone could keep track of the number of elms he sees while another could count oaks.
- What **season** is it? Should the children look for new shoots and buds swelling on the trees? Or are the trees losing their leaves in preparation for winter? Do *all* trees lose their leaves? What do **dormant** and **deciduous** mean? How is losing its leaves actually a way the tree has of preserving its life?
- Depending on where you walk, you may see **insects**. How is an insect like a person and other forms of animal life? Does it breathe, eat, sleep, have babies? How is it different? What kind of eyes does it have? How many legs does it have? Do you have wings? Where is its skeleton? What is an **exoskeleton**? What about its young—do they have the same body type regardless of size, or do they change form? What is a **larva**? A **pupa**? Does an insect shed its skin? Do you?
- Perhaps your walk will give you a chance to see some **animals**. What must animals have to live? How are their needs for shelter, food, and water like those of people? How are they different? Why are animals and birds found more frequently where two types of vegetation meet, such as at the edge of a meadow beside a forest? Why are more animals and birds seen at dawn and dusk than at any other time of day?

8

183

- Notice the **birds**. What birds are scavengers, clean-up experts, watchmen, smart, stupid, brave, shy, big, little, quiet, talkative? Their "vocalizing" ranges from melodic song to harsh croak. Can you name some birds and describe or classify their song? What materials do they use in building their nests?
- If you are walking near **water**, consider living things that can be found in water. What do they eat? How do they protect themselves? How are they built to live in the water?

While on your walk, leave natural sites undisturbed. Dispose of your litter properly, and collect specimens only if you have permission to do so. If you are walking in a rugged area through which there are marked trails, stay on them and caution children to do the same. For this type of walking, wear sturdy oxfords or hiking boots to protect your feet and ankles. To avoid bites and possible rabies infection, make no effort to feed or handle wild animals. Become familiar with irritant or poisonous plants, such as poison ivy and poison oak, if they are likely to be found where you are walking and help children learn how to identify and avoid them.

Should you have to cancel your walk because of bad weather, remember that **weather** is also a natural phenomenon worthy of observation, even if it must be through a window.

- You might want to talk about clouds, fog, rain, thunder, lightning, hail, snow, sleet, wind, hurricanes, tornadoes.
- What is **precipitation**?

CAMPING

A camping experience, whether for one night or for one week, can give your children a chance not only to look at nature but also to live with it. You can enrich this experience for them by providing opportunities for

1. Experiencing democratic social living. Children learn the skills associated with group planning, group responsibility, self-expression, dances, and games. They practice social graces and manners and experience leadership, followership, and fellowship.
2. Increasing scientific appreciation and understanding. Children learn to identify plants and animals. They study stars, rock formations, animal tracking, insects, soil erosion, conservation, sanitation, and weather.
3. Learning about healthful living and safety. Children study the water supply, swimming

and life saving, and survival techniques. They learn to prepare food, to build and put out a camp fire, to use and care for camping tools and equipment. They learn about sanitation and safety procedures.
4. Taking part in purposeful work experiences. Children can gather and cut wood, build fires, cook and serve food, wash dishes, clean cabins, and care for animals. They can clear and mark trails, help in camp beautification, and police campgrounds.
5. Acquiring and refining recreational skills by dancing, singing, swimming, hiking, making handicraft items, and taking part in campfire programs and storytelling.
6. Enriching spiritual values through campfire fellowship and the discovery and appreciation of beauty in nature.

CRAFTS

Most children take great pride in, and derive considerable satisfaction from, creating something with their own hands. And crafts projects make excellent indoor activities for wet, cold, hot, or smoggy days.

Materials for crafts need not be expensive. Much can be done with inexpensive items, "leftovers," and things that might otherwise be thrown away. Consider the crafts possibilities in

- beans and seeds of assorted sizes, shapes, and colors
- emptied cans, bottles, or jars
- empty thread spools
- nuts and nut shells
- pasta of assorted shapes
- pipe cleaners
- seashells
- sequins and glitter
- toothpicks
- yarn, ribbon, and fabric scraps

Crafts projects can be structured or unstructured; that is, you can give children specific directions about how to assemble, from materials provided, an item you or someone else has previously designed, or you can give them the material and let them do the designing. Either approach is valid, and your choice should depend on the time and materials available, the capabilities of your children, and the end result you and the children desire. On the pages that follow are directions for several crafts projects. No doubt you'll want to add to them many other project ideas of your own.

8

PASTA PAINTING

Materials: Empty tin can, bottle, jar, or plastic container
Cement glue
Spray paint
Pasta of various shapes and sizes
Spray varnish

Directions:

- Pasta may be spray painted different colors or put on unpainted. If sprayed several colors, allow the paint to dry, then glue the pasta on the container with cement.
- If using pasta of one color, glue first, then allow to dry before spraying the entire container.
- Varnish when the glue and paint are thoroughly dry.
- Use the container as a vase or planter, or to hold pencils, paint brushes, dried flowers, etc.

8

185

DECORATIVE HANGING OR BANNER

Materials: Piece of fabric
Felt of assorted colors
Glue
Dowel rods (optional)

Directions:
- Cut felt into desired shapes.
- Glue shapes on fabric in desired pattern.
- If resulting picture is to be hung on wall, hand or machine stitch each end and insert dowels.

SHELL BOAT

Materials: Walnut   Glue
Wooden matches   Paint or varnish
Paper   Small hand drill

Directions:
- Cut walnut in half and clean out the shell.
- Drill holes and insert match for cross bar.
- Orient a second match vertically, gluing it to the cross bar and the bottom of the shell to form the mast.
- Cut sails from paper and glue them to the mast.
- Varnish or paint the boat.

NUTTY ANIMALS

Materials: Pecans, small and large | Bottle cork or pecan shell halves
Flat toothpicks | for duck's base
Wooden matches | Construction paper or felt scraps
Pipe cleaners | for eyes
Glue | Small hand drill

Directions:

DUCK

- Select a small pecan for the head and draw or glue eyes on it.
- Drill holes in the small pecan for the neck and beak.
- Drill holes in the large pecan for the neck and tail.
- Insert a match for the neck, pipe cleaners for the tail, and toothpicks for the beak.
- Glue the duck to the base.

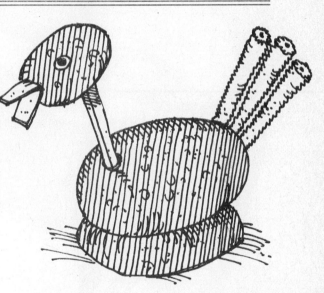

RABBIT

- Select a small pecan for the head and draw or glue eyes on it.
- Drill holes in the small pecan for the ears.
- Drill holes in the large pecan for the legs and tail.
- Form the legs, ears, and tail from pipe cleaners, using glue as needed to hold parts in place.
- Glue head to body.

Note:

If you wish, you can drill holes for the front legs only and simply glue the hind legs and the tail to the body.

187

THE BUILDING BLOCKS OF PHYSICAL LIFE

9.

Most children grow up without learning about how their bodies grow, work, and play, and how they can best be maintained. Yet such knowledge should be a part of every child's education. And the earlier in life this learning occurs, the greater the opportunity for its use to direct or even correct development and to achieve health and happiness.

Why not learn to identify parts of the body as soon as possible?

These beginning "building blocks" have been arranged so that the pages may be removed and placed on a bulletin board or even reproduced for individual study. The first building block contains elementary information about the human body.

THE HUMAN CELL

The **cell** is the body's basic structural unit. Every part of the body is composed of millions of tiny cells. There are skin cells, muscle cells, blood cells, nerve cells, and bone cells. Each varies in size and shape, depending upon the tissue it composes and the function it performs. Every cell is capable of reproducing itself, and it is through this process of cell reproduction (usually **mitosis**) that the body grows and that damaged or worn out cells are replaced.

Each cell requires food and oxygen and must have its waste products removed so that it will not be poisoned by them. Exercise stimulates blood circulation and thus the feeding of the cells and the removal of their waste products. Inadequate food, water, oxygen, or rest may cause cells to become sick.

Similar cells are grouped together to form **tissues**. There are four basic kinds of tissue in everyone:

- **epithelial**—comprises the skin and covers the openings in the body
- **connective**—holds different parts of the body together
- **nervous**—forms the communications network on which messages are sent throughout the body
- **muscle**—on which all movement depends

Two or more tissues grouped together to perform certain functions are called **organs**. Some of your body's organs are the heart, lungs, brain, eyes, liver, kidneys, stomach, and intestines. Each organ has a very special job to do and can do its job best when it is healthy. The health of all tissues and organs depends upon nutrition, exercise, and freedom from disease.

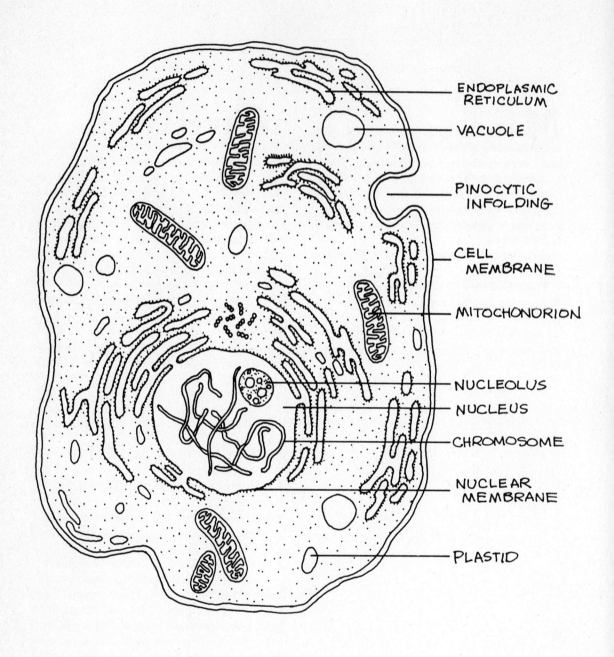

ENDOPLASMIC
RETICULUM

VACUOLE

PINOCYTIC
INFOLDING

CELL
MEMBRANE

MITOCHONDRION

NUCLEOLUS
NUCLEUS

CHROMOSOME

NUCLEAR
MEMBRANE

PLASTID

THE HUMAN CELL

9

SYSTEMS

A **system** is an arrangement of organs concerned with the same function. The major systems of the body are:

- **skeletal** (bones)
- **muscular** (muscles)
- **cardiovascular** (heart, arteries, veins, blood)
- **lymphatic** (lymph, lymph nodes and vessels)
- **endocrine** (a number of ductless glands)
- **respiratory** (lungs)
- **nervous** (brain and nerves)
- **digestive** (alimentary canal and its accessories)
- **reproductive** (organs used in making new life)

All of these systems work together to keep the body alive and functioning properly.

THE SKELETAL SYSTEM

The human body is composed of some 206 bones termed **axial** (skull, backbone, and ribs) or **appendicular** (arms, legs, hips, and shoulders). The total human bone framework or skeleton supports the soft tissues and protects the delicate organs, such as the heart, spinal cord, lungs, and brain.

Bones also serve as levers for movement. They are primarily a dense form of connective tissue. The inorganic material—chiefly calcium phosphate—they contain makes them hard, while the protein in them gives them their flexibility. Strong, healthy bones depend upon sufficient exercise and upon adequate calcium in the diet. Milk is a good source of calcium, as are almonds, cheese, and leafy vegetables.

Related Activities:

- If possible, obtain (perhaps from your butcher or from a can of salmon) some bones and examine them. Note particularly their texture and strength and the way vertebrae fit together to form the backbone or spine.
- What is a bone break called? (A fracture.) How are bones broken? How can you avoid this type of injury? How does a doctor determine that a bone is broken? What does he do to help it heal properly?
- If possible, obtain and look at X-rays of healthy, broken, and healed bones.
- Do insects have a skeleton?
- What is a **vertebrate?** An **invertebrate?**
- What would you study in **osteology?**
- What is **ossification?**
- If we say someone's mind has **ossified,** what do we mean? (That it has become hardened or resistant to new ideas.)
- Where is the smallest bone in the human body? (Inside the ear.)
- Where is the largest bone in the human body? (In the thigh.) What is it called? (The **femur**.)

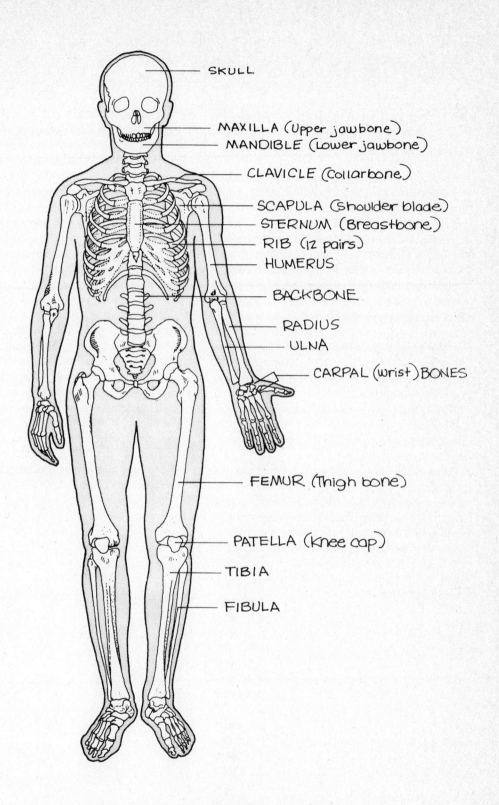

SKULL

MAXILLA (Upper jawbone)
MANDIBLE (Lower jawbone)

CLAVICLE (Collarbone)

SCAPULA (Shoulder blade)
STERNUM (Breastbone)
RIB (12 pairs)
HUMERUS

BACKBONE

RADIUS
ULNA

CARPAL (Wrist) BONES

FEMUR (Thigh bone)

PATELLA (Knee cap)

TIBIA

FIBULA

THE SKELETAL SYSTEM

THE MUSCULAR SYSTEM

The human body is composed of some 650 to 700 separate muscles that make up 40 to 60 percent of its total weight. These muscles may be divided into three types:

- **skeletal**—are voluntary and move the body
- **smooth**—are involuntary and form the walls of all internal organs and surround the intestines and blood vessels
- **cardiac**—is involuntary and forms the heart

Muscles cannot push: they can only pull, and in doing so, they shorten or contract. To enable skeletal or voluntary muscles to reverse the moves they make, they are usually arranged in pairs or combinations such as that, for instance, one group pulls the arm forward and up and another group pulls it backward and up. Groups of muscles working together to perform a task are called **synergist**. Those acting in opposition are called **antagonist**.

Within the body, various groups of neighboring muscles work together. Such muscle groups are those of the chest, back, arms, legs, neck, face, foot, and the organs.

Strong muscles are needed to fight off the pull of gravity, to resist fatigue, to look healthy, to move gracefully, to become skilled in sports, and to be a winner in life. Exercise stimulates muscle growth, while the lack of it causes a muscle to diminish in size and strength (**atropy**). Protein is the main cell and muscle builder. It is found in meat, fish, poultry, eggs, milk, cheese, peas, beans, and nuts.

Related Activities:

- Talk about muscles. How can you tell a muscle is growing stronger? Can anyone develop larger muscles? What kinds of exercise promote most muscle growth? How often should you exercise? Does vigorous play stimulate muscle growth?
- What kinds of work can you do around your home to promote muscle growth? Would a hand- or motor-powered lawn mower provide more exercise? When doing errands for your parents, would walking or running provide more exercise?
- What is a muscle cramp? What causes such a cramp? (E.g., chilling, an inadequate supply of blood to the muscle.) What can you do to relieve the pain and stiffness associated with a cramp? (E.g., warm and massage the affected muscle to stimulate the flow of blood to it; stretch it if possible to "loosen" the cramp.)
- What is a "Charley horse"? Did you ever have one?
- Do some of the Lifting Activities on page 23.
- With a partner, One-Arm Wrestle as described on page 122.

9

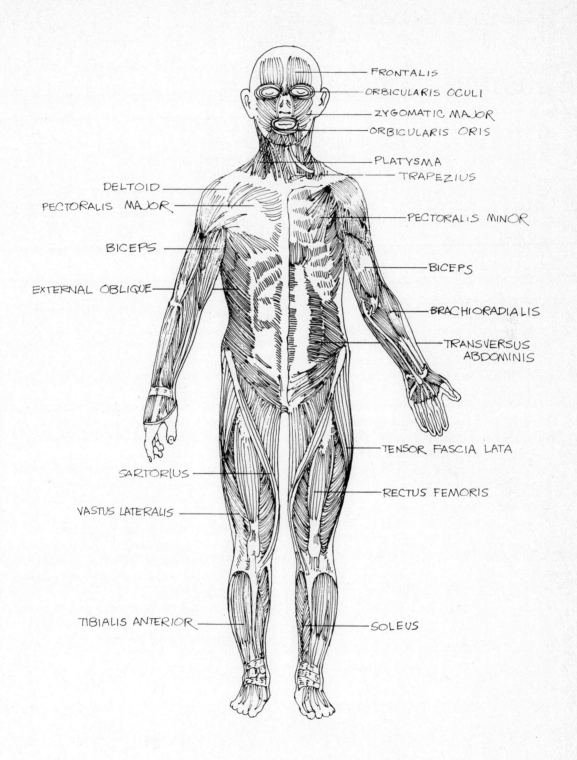

FRONTALIS
ORBICULARIS OCULI
ZYGOMATIC MAJOR
ORBICULARIS ORIS
PLATYSMA
TRAPEZIUS
DELTOID
PECTORALIS MAJOR
PECTORALIS MINOR
BICEPS
BICEPS
EXTERNAL OBLIQUE
BRACHIORADIALIS
TRANSVERSUS ABDOMINIS
TENSOR FASCIA LATA
SARTORIUS
RECTUS FEMORIS
VASTUS LATERALIS
TIBIALIS ANTERIOR
SOLEUS

THE MUSCULAR SYSTEM

POSTURE

Posture is the relative arrangement or position of different parts of the body. **Good posture** keeps all body organs in the position in which they function best and are not crowded by other organs or restricted in their movement. When standing, the head should be held up with the chin slightly tucked. The chest should be raised as if lifted by a string attached to the breastbone (**sternum**), the abdomen should be flat, and the curves of the back should be within normal limits. A straight line drawn vertically should pass through the ear, shoulder, hip, and ankle.

Poor posture is usually caused by muscle weakness or laziness. Among recognized postural defects are lordosis, kyphosis, and scoliosis. **Lordosis** is abnormal forward curvature of the spine. **Kyphosis**, on the other hand, is abnormal backward curvature of the spine. **Scoliosis**, from the Greek word *skoliosis* meaning crookedness, is lateral curvature of the spine. While these conditions are sometimes congenital, they are often the result of inadequate muscle development or muscle imbalance and may be corrected by carefully prescribed exercises.

Related Activities:

- Talk about the relationship between good posture and good balance.
- Try or review the Walking Activities on page 15, Balance and Reverse on page 86, Balance Beam Activities on page 98, and the Balance Beam Routine on page 125.
- Use a full-length mirror to enable children to assess their posture while walking, standing, sitting, and lifting.
- If possible, take photographs or motion pictures of children for posture evaluation. This might become a "before" and "after" activity where photographs are taken at the beginning of the year and again after children have been made aware of their posture and have participated in some posture-developing exercises and activities.
- If photographs are out of the question, use a strong light source to cast each child's shadow on white butcher or construction paper and make posture silhouettes.
- Talk about or list occupations in which good posture obviously contributes to success (e.g., being a model, a tightrope walker, a ballet dancer).
- Talk about or list occupations that tend to encourage the development of poor posture by requiring that people stand or sit uncomfortably or bend awkwardly for long periods (e.g., picking cotton).
- Discuss the way furniture that is properly constructed contributes to the development and maintenance of good posture.

9

GOOD POSTURE

THE CARDIOVASCULAR SYSTEM

The **cardiovascular system** includes the **heart, arteries, veins,** and **blood**. Each person has five to six quarts of blood in his body. The heart, which is about the size of a clinched fist, pumps this blood through the arteries into the capillaries and back through the veins to the heart. During rest, the blood makes one complete journey around the body each minute. During exercise, it may make nine trips in the same amount of time.

The arteries, veins, and capillaries are called **blood vessels**. They are tubes and hoses of varying size through which the body's blood is pumped. If all the blood vessels in one adult human body were hooked end-to-end, they would extend thousands of miles!

The heart is composed of four chambers, the left and right **auricles** and the left and right **ventricles. Valves** within the heart control the flow of blood between the chambers.

The blood is made up of red blood cells, white blood cells, platelets, and plasma.

- **Red blood cells**, produced in the bone marrow, carry oxygen and carbon dioxide between the tissues and the lungs.
- **White blood cells**, produced in the bone marrow, the thymus, the spleen, and the lymph nodes, defend the body against infection.
- **Platelets**, disc-shaped blood corpuscles, repair damaged vessels and aid in the blood clotting process.
- **Plasma**, a water-like substance, makes up 50 percent of the blood. It carries nutrients to all cells, removes water products, and acts as a cooling system during exercise.

The development of strong skeletal muscles through exercise usually results in a strong cardiovascular system.

Related Activities:

- Help children feel their pulse in a superficial artery of the wrist or neck. Explain that what they are feeling is the ventricles' strong contraction, what we call the **heartbeat**. Record and compare pulse rates for different children before and after vigorous activity. Normal rates before activity are:

for a baby	130 beats per minute
for a ten-year-old	90 beats per minute
for an adult woman	78 beats per minute
for an adult man	70 beats per minute
for a long-distance runner	50 beats per minute

- If possible, borrow a stethoscope and help each child listen to his own heartbeat.

- Talk about pumps. What kinds of pumps are there? How do they work? Why are pumps needed? Why can't we rely on water and other liquids to flow down or up, wherever they are needed or wanted? Why does the circulatory system need a pump?

- What happens to the relative distribution of blood throughout the body when you stand on your head, hang by your knees, or otherwise remain for a time with your head below heart level? Why might sitting with his head between his knees help someone who feels dizzy or faint?

- Talk about first aid and the importance of stopping or controlling bleeding. Mention that the flow of blood from minor cuts on the arms and legs can often be slowed to permit natural clotting by elevating the affected part of the body above heart level (i.e., raising your hand over your head or lying down with your leg elevated).

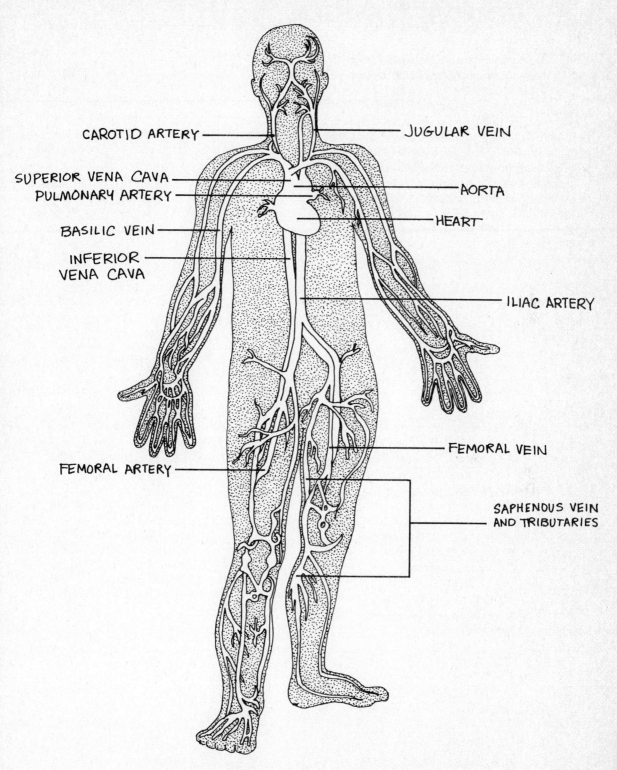

CAROTID ARTERY

JUGULAR VEIN

SUPERIOR VENA CAVA

PULMONARY ARTERY

AORTA

BASILIC VEIN

HEART

INFERIOR
VENA CAVA

ILIAC ARTERY

FEMORAL VEIN

FEMORAL ARTERY

SAPHENOUS VEIN
AND TRIBUTARIES

THE CARDIOVASCULAR SYSTEM

THE LYMPHATIC SYSTEM

The **lymphatic system** is a system of vessels that carry lymph throughout the body. **Lymph** is a watery fluid that drains from the blood vessels and tissues, carrying away waste materials. Little glands called **lymph nodes** serve as filters for this system. As the lymph passes through them, they trap and destroy harmful bacteria. The cleaned lymph is then returned to the bloodstream. The lymphatic system has no pump, but relies instead on body motion to circulate lymph through its vessels.

9

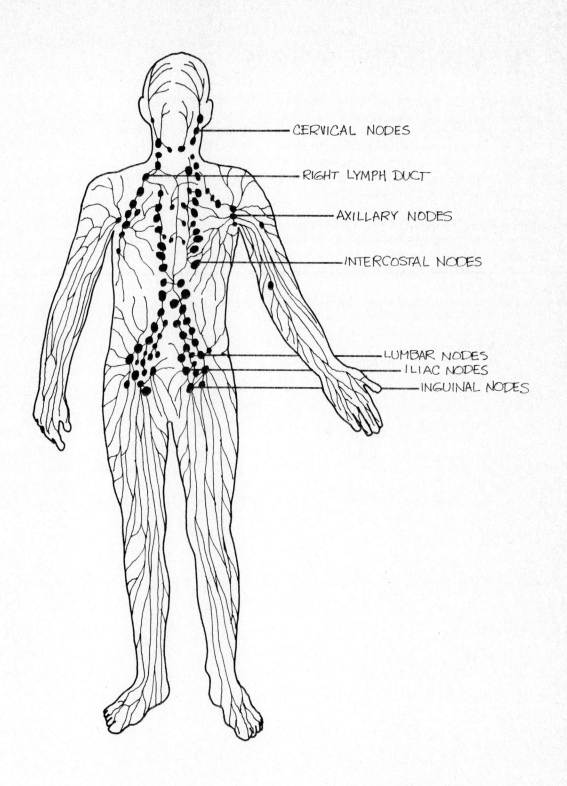

CERVICAL NODES

RIGHT LYMPH DUCT

AXILLARY NODES

INTERCOSTAL NODES

LUMBAR NODES
ILIAC NODES
INGUINAL NODES

THE LYMPHATIC SYSTEM

THE ENDOCRINE SYSTEM

The **endocrine system** consists of ductless glands located in the head, neck, and torso. These glands make and secrete chemical substances called **hormones** that regulate the work of various body organs. Among these glands are:

- the **pituitary**, the master ductless gland, which controls all other glands and regulates body growth.
- the **thyroid**, which regulates body temperature and determines how quickly the body uses up food and oxygen.
- the **parathyroid**, which controls body metabolism.
- the **pancreas**, which produces **insulin**, a substance that helps the muscles convert sugar to energy.
- the **adrenal glands**, which produce **adrenalin**, a substance that speeds up the heartbeat and gives the body added energy in an emergency.
- the **sex glands** or **gonads** (**ovaries** in girls and **testes** in boys), which stimulate the development of sex specific physical characteristics and are used in reproduction.

Related Activities:

- What is a **duct**?
- If these glands are **ductless**, how do the hormones get out of the glands to do their work in the body?
- What is **osmosis**?

9

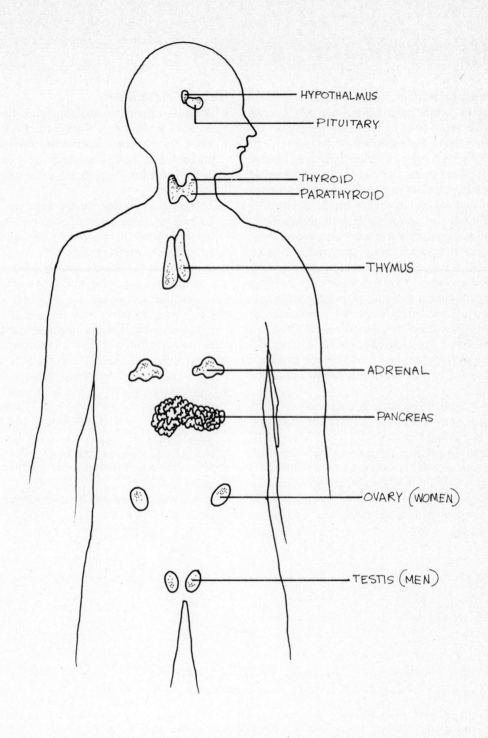

THE ENDOCRINE SYSTEM

THE RESPIRATORY SYSTEM

The **respiratory system** includes the **nose, trachea, larynx,** and **lungs**. Its major responsibilities are to bring **oxygen** into the body and to remove **carbon dioxide** from it.

Oxygen is brought into the body in air inhaled through the nose. The hairs and sticky mucous lining of the nose trap dust and other particles that may be in the air so that they do not damage the lungs. The myriad tiny blood vessels in the nose warm the inhaled air as it passes over them so that it is close to body temperature when it enters the lungs.

The exchange of carbon dioxide for oxygen is accomplished in the lungs. The lungs are subdivided into millions of very small, balloon-like air sacs. A network of tiny blood vessels surrounds each air sac. Through these vessels, oxygen passes to the red blood cells, and carbon dioxide is removed from them to be breathed out of the body.

Underneath the lungs is a muscle called the **diaphragm**. When you inhale, it contracts, pulling the ribs up and making room for more air. As you relax to exhale, the rib cage becomes smaller, lung capacity is reduced, and air within the lungs is forced out. When you are sitting still, this process takes place about 18 times each minute. During exercise, it occurs much more frequently.

Related Activities:

- What do **inhale** and **exhale** mean? Demonstrate each one.
- What do the words **expiration, inspiration, perspiration,** and **respiration** have in common? Look them up to see what each one means.
- Talk about how delicate the lungs are, how easily they can be damaged, and how the respiratory system is designed to filter and heat inhaled air to protect them.
- Explain that the body's natural defenses are inadequate against the inhalation of cigarette smoke, polluted air, etc.
- Talk about pollution. How does air become polluted? What are the principal sources of pollutants in the air? What natural objects help clean and purify the air? (Green plants.) What effect does severe air pollution have on them?
- Talk about diseases of the lungs and respiratory system, such as asthma, bronchitis, cancer, emphysema, pneumonia, and tuberculosis. How does each one affect the lungs' ability to do their essential work in the body? How can they be prevented, detected, and treated?
- Talk about posture and its relationship to lung capacity.

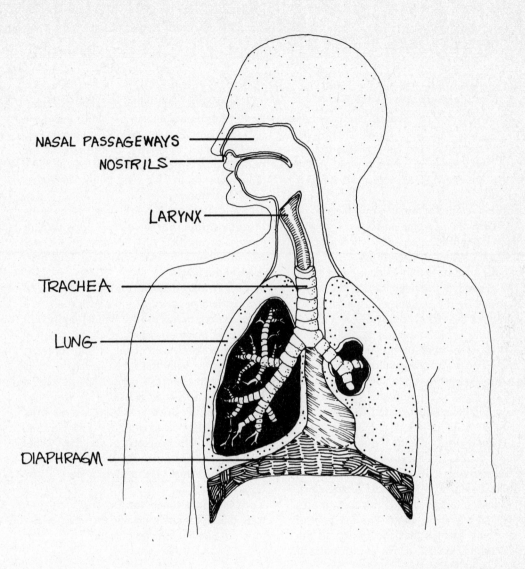

NASAL PASSAGEWAYS

NOSTRILS

LARYNX

TRACHEA

LUNG

DIAPHRAGM

THE RESPIRATORY SYSTEM

9

205

THE NERVOUS SYSTEM

The **nervous system** consists of the **brain**, the **spinal cord**, and the **nerves**.

The brain is a complicated communications center. It receives impulses from all parts of the body, deciphers them, and either stores the information they contain or sends a reply to the body to do something. The three main parts of the brain are:

- **cerebrum**—center of thinking and feeling
- **cerebellum**—helps move muscles
- **medulla**—controls automatic body functions, including breathing and heartbeat

The spinal cord, a half-inch-thick cable, runs from the brain all the way down the back through holes in the vertebrae. Two kinds of nerves connect the spinal cord with parts of the body. One kind carries messages from the brain through the spinal cord to the body and the other kind carries messages from the body through the cord to the brain. Some messages do not go all the way to the brain. Instead, they result in a **reflex action** initiated in the spinal cord.

The nervous system may be thought of as two subsystems, the **central nervous system** and the **autonomic nervous system**. The central nervous system controls all voluntary movements, while the autonomic system controls movements you don't have to think about, like the beat of your heart, the breaths that you take, and the reflex actions that quickly move you or parts of your body away from pain or danger.

Related Activities:

- Talk about the brain. How does the skull protect it? Are there joints in the skull? What is a baby's soft spot? Is the human brain relatively large or small compared to the size of the body it directs and controls? What about a dinosaur's brain? Do you think dinosaurs were very smart?
- Talk about nerves. Name several places in the human body that are very sensitive to touch—or are ticklish—because of a heavy concentration of nerve ends (e.g., fingertips, soles of the feet).
- What is **Braille**? How is it used?
- Untwist two paper clips and attach them to a ruler (perhaps with rubber bands) an inch or two apart. Have one child touch some part of another child's body (back, neck, forearm, palm) lightly with this "sensometer." How close together can the paper clips be placed before it is no longer possible to "feel" two distinct points? Does this distance vary from one part of the body to another? From boys to girls? From one person to another? What might this distance indicate about the number of nerve endings in a particular part of the body?
- Conduct some touch tests in which children wear blindfolds and must rely on their sense of touch to identify familiar objects.

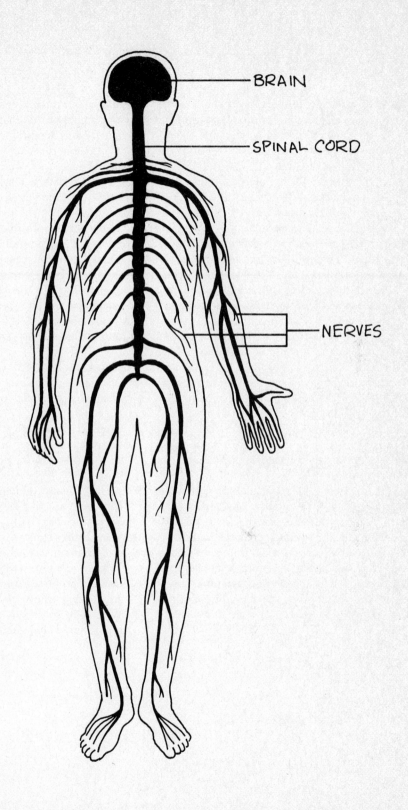

BRAIN

SPINAL CORD

NERVES

THE NERVOUS SYSTEM

9

THE DIGESTIVE SYSTEM

The **digestive system** includes the **mouth, esophagus, stomach, small intestine**, and **large intestine**, which form a long tube extending from the mouth to the **anus** or **rectum**. The system's function is to take in food and water, make them usable for body growth and repair, and eliminate the waste products. This food processing is called **digestion**.

Digestion begins in the mouth. Your sharp **teeth** (incisors and cuspids) bite off pieces of food. Your broader, flatter teeth (bicuspids and molars) chew and grind it. As your teeth chew your food, three sets of **salivary glands** in your mouth secrete **saliva** to moisten the food and help you taste it. **Taste buds** located on your tongue tell you whether the food is sweet, sour, bitter, or salty. Your sense of smell tells you it's fried chicken!

During the chewing process, your **tongue** moves the food around in your mouth, then pushes it to the back of your mouth to be swallowed. Swallowed food goes down the esophagus into the stomach. Located under your ribs on the left side of your abdomen, the stomach is like a J-shaped balloon made of tough muscle rather than rubber. **Sphincter muscles** close both stomach openings so that food will not be squeezed back up into the esophagus or down into the small intestine before it is ready. Glands in the stomach walls secrete digestive juices. These juices contain special chemical substances called **enzymes** that are mixed with the food by the squeezing action of the stomach-wall muscles and aid in breaking it down.

After about three hours, the sphincter leading to the small intestine opens, and contracting stomach muscles push the food into the intestinal tract. Together, the small and large intestines are about 30 feet long. They have to be coiled up like a garden hose to fit within your body. Strong muscles developed through daily exercise aid in pushing food along in the intestines.

In the small intestine, additional digestive juices from the **liver, gall bladder**, and **pancreas** are added, muscles continue mixing and pushing the food, and tiny blood vessels absorb useful food particles into the bloodstream. The large intestine absorbs any useful liquid remaining in the food mixture and eliminates what is left through the rectum as semisolid waste.

Related Activities:

- Why does food lose its "taste" when your nose is "stopped up" as the result of a cold or allergies?
- Conduct some taste tests in which children wear blindfolds and hold their noses (briefly) so that they are forced to rely on their taste buds alone. (*Note:* A bite of bland cracker or a swish of water will help eliminate residual effects from an old taste so that a new one can be appreciated.)
- Using simple substances (e.g., table sugar and salt, a lemon slice, and an orange peel), help children identify sweet, salty, sour, and bitter tastes. Can they distinguish between salt and sugar using taste alone?
- Why is it unwise to exercise vigorously or swim shortly after eating a large meal?

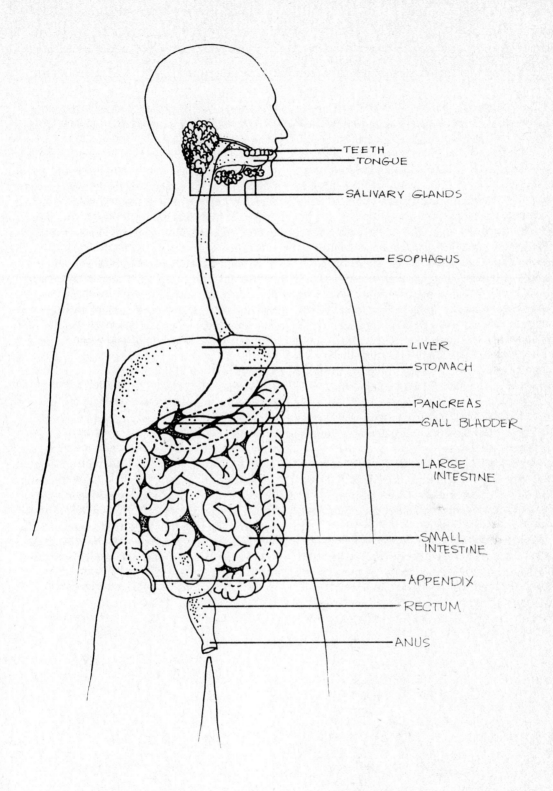

TEETH
TONGUE
SALIVARY GLANDS
ESOPHAGUS
LIVER
STOMACH
PANCREAS
GALL BLADDER
LARGE INTESTINE
SMALL INTESTINE
APPENDIX
RECTUM
ANUS

THE DIGESTIVE SYSTEM

NUTRITION

Many American children are overweight, many are malnourished, and some are both! Malnourished children may have pale skin, dull-looking hair, circles under their eyes, flabby or stringy muscles, a flat chest, thin arms and legs, and poor posture. They often find it difficult to concentrate and frequently fall victim to colds and skin infections. In many instances, obesity and malnutrition share the same cause: ignorance or a nutrient negligence that maintains it doesn't matter what you fill the stomach with so long as you do fill it at regular intervals.

The truth is, the body's needs are simple but specific: if bones are being built or repaired, calcium is needed, and carbohydrates will *not* do equally well—will not do at all! Children should learn early what the body's nutritional needs are so they can make wise food choices to better meet the needs of their own bodies as they grow and develop.

The body's basic nutrients may be divided into five categories: proteins, carbohydrates, fats, vitamins, and minerals.

Protein is essential to building and maintaining each body cell. In addition, it aids in the development of antibodies which help the body resist disease. Meat, eggs, and milk products are good sources of protein.

Carbohydrates supply energy for work and play. If one's diet lacks carbohydrates, the body will use proteins for energy rather than for cell building and repair. Carbohydrates are found in breads, cereals, fruits, sweets, potatoes, and some other vegetables.

Fats are used both as fuel and as insulation to help the body maintain a normal temperature (98.6°). The fat content of food is often measured in calories, a unit that expresses the energy- or heat-producing value of the food. Bacon, cream, butter, and some meats are good sources of fat.

Vitamins are chemical substances found in both animal and vegetable matter. In general, they promote normal growth, maintain health, and prevent and/or cure certain diseases. An adequate daily supply of vitamins may be obtained by eating a variety of basic foods, such as:

- leafy green and yellow vegetables
- citrus fruits and tomatoes
- potatoes and fruits
- cheese and milk
- meat, fish, poultry, eggs, and legumes
- butter and margarine
- breads and cereals

Minerals help the body resist infections, promote the healing of wounds, and aid in curing various illnesses. They are essential for building strong bones and teeth, and for having a good appetite. The main minerals needed by the body are calcium, phosphorous, and iron, which are found in most leafy green vegetables, fruits, liver, and kidneys.

THE BODY'S VITAMIN AND MINERAL NEEDS

Name	Source	Function in the Body	Servings Daily
Vitamin A	Butter, cheese, cod liver oil, egg yolk, leafy green vegetables, liver, yellow vegetables, and tomatoes	Promotes normal vision and growth; maintains general health	One
Vitamin B Complex	Lean pork, liver, egg yolk, whole grains, beans, peas, nuts, fruits, vegetables	Stimulates appetite; aids digestion; promotes growth; regulates nervous system	Two
Vitamin C	Citrus fruits, other fresh fruits, berries, cabbage, greens, fresh vegetables, sprouted legumes	Maintains connective tissue; assists in the development of bones and teeth; aids cell activity; strengthens blood vessels and body tissues	Two (cannot be stored)
Vitamin D	Eggs, liver, fish, sunshine	Essential for bone and teeth development; promotes growth	One
Vitamin E	Egg yolk, cereals, lettuce, spinach, corn oil	Promotes general well-being, mental and physical vigor, good muscle tone	One
Calcium	Almonds, cheese, dry beans, egg yolk, milk, leafy vegetables, molasses	Assists in the development of bones and teeth; aids blood clotting; essential for healthy muscles and nerves	Two
Copper	Avocadoes, dry beans, peas, liver, oats, corn, whole wheat	Aids cell activity; prevents certain anemias	One
Iodine	Seafoods, fish, foods grown near the ocean, iodized salt	Encourages normal growth; prevents goiter	One
Iron	Berries, fruits, dried fruits, dried beans, peas, eggs, lean meats, bread, green vegetables, molasses, rye flour, whole wheat, oatmeal	Builds hemoglobin and other carriers of oxygen; prevents some anemias	One
Phosphorus	Cheese, dried beans, liver, nuts, flour	Stimulates and aids cell activity; assists in the development of bones and teeth	One
Potassium	Dried apricots, dates, figs, dried beans, molasses, nuts, soy flour	Promotes growth; stimulates and aids cell activity; essential for healthy heart, nerves, and muscles	One
Sodium	Bread, butter, cheese, salmon, table salt	Helps maintain water balance; prevents fatigue	One

9

DISEASES

A **disease** is an abnormal condition of an organism as a consequence of infection, inherent weakness, or environmental factors which impairs normal functioning. Some diseases, such as pellagra, rickets, and scurvy, are caused by deficiencies of certain vitamins and minerals. Other diseases, such as colds, measles, mumps, and chicken pox, are caused by germs.

Germs or **microbes** destroy body cells and produce poisons that can make the body very sick. They are especially dangerous because, once inside the body, they grow and reproduce rapidly. Some become full-grown within a few minutes. Among these disease-causing organisms are bacteria, protozoa, and viruses.

Bacteria are one-celled microorganisms found everywhere. Most of them are harmless and are essential for plant growth; however, a few of them cause infections, blood poisoning, food spoilage, pneumonia, whooping cough, typhoid, and scarlet fever.

Protozoa are tiny animals that live in the water. Most of them are helpful, but a few cause diseases such as malaria and sleeping sickness.

Viruses are submicroscopic bacteria or fungi that cause colds, influenza, measles, mumps, chicken pox, and polio. Diseases caused by viruses do not respond well to medication and are, for the most part, easier to prevent than to cure.

Resistance to germs may be developed by
- getting plenty of rest, exercising, and eating the correct foods;
- keeping clean and treating all wounds;
- washing your hands before eating;
- keeping warm and dry, avoiding becoming chilled;
- staying away from people who are sick;
- drinking only purified liquids and eating only unspoiled foods;
- visiting your doctor and dentist regularly for checkups and following their advice.

Disease is spread most often
- person to person by coughs or sneezes;
- by insects, such as flies, cockroaches, and mosquitos, or by fungi;
- by the bite of an infected animal (dog, cat, or parasite);
- by drinking unpastuerized milk or polluted water, or by eating meat from an infected animal;
- by human carriers who are immune to the disease's effects and so may not know they are carrying it.

THE BODY'S DEFENSES

The body's defenses include its covering, its white blood cells, and its temperature. The **skin** is the body's first line of defense. It should be kept clean; breaks in it, such as scratches and cuts, should be cleansed and treated with an antiseptic solution. If deep or extensive, they should also be covered. The **white blood cells** form a second line of defense: they surround and destroy germs. Another of the body's defenses is **temperature elevation:** some bacteria cannot live at the high temperatures we call a fever and thus are destroyed.

In response to infection or exposure to disease, the body may develop **antibodies,** chemical substances within the bloodstream that kill invading germs. The production of antibodies within the body can be stimulated by the injection of **antigens** or **haptens,** that is, by "shots" or vaccination.

If the disease is prolonged or severe, or the body's defenses prove inadequate, the doctor may need to give medicine to help the body fight off the germs' effects.

SAFETY AND ACCIDENT PREVENTION

Every year thousands of children lose their lives, are permanently injured, or miss time from school because of accidents. To prevent accidents, anticipate them and take corrective action before they happen.

1. Develop safety patrols to prevent jaywalking, dashing into the street, crossing the streets outside crosswalks, and playing in unsafe areas. See that traffic in corridors or on stairways moves in an orderly fashion.

2. Provide instruction on where and how to use roller skates, skate boards, scooters, and bicycles, and where to store them.

3. Inspect daily for maintenance defects and housekeeping carelessness in buildings and play areas. Among other things, check
   - exit lights
   - exit door locks
   - electrical connections
   - fire extinguishers
   - stair treads and handrails (Are there splinters or exposed nails?)
   - floors (Are they slippery?)
   - playground equipment

4. Encourage everyone to report all accidents on an accident report form and to list the probable cause. Follow up on all probable causes to assure that remedial action is taken so that the same accident will not recur.

5. Have readily available *all* telephone numbers that might be needed in an emergency, such as those of the
   - fire department
   - physician
   - nurse
   - emergency hospital
   - parents or guardians at home and at work

6. Conduct regular fire, safety, and disaster drills. Discuss with children *exactly* what they should do in such emergencies, and in what order.

7. All games have dangerous elements. Teach children how to avoid being hit, being run into, or running into someone; how to fall; and how to protect themselves by being alert to dangers and by raising their hands, tucking, ducking, or taking other evasive action. Teach them not to throw bats, masks, or other equipment, or rocks, bottles, sticks, and other objects.

8. Encourage children to be safety conscious and to correct or report dangerous situations they observe (e.g., a busy intersection where a traffic light or crossing guard is needed, a loose rung or bar on playground equipment, broken glass or other sharp objects scattered about a play area).

CONCLUSION

The human body is a miraculous structure in which many diverse building blocks are combined to make possible work and play. The simplest of these blocks is the **cell**. Within the body, cells are combined to make **tissues**, tissues to make **organs**, and organs to make **systems**. All nine of the body's major systems work together to keep it alive and functioning properly. Children need to learn early how to nourish, exercise, and relax their bodies and how to protect them from accidents and disease. Adults who work with children have an inescapable responsibility to teach these lessons through study and activity, and by example.

BIBLIOGRAPHY

Anderson, M. H., et al., *Play with a Purpose* (New York: Harper and Row, 1966).

Braga, Laurie, and Joseph Braga, *Learning and Growing: A Guide to Child Development* (Englewood Cliffs, N.J.: Prentice-Hall, 1975).

Byrd, O. E., et al., *Health-6: Health, Safety, Fitness* (Sacramento: California State Department of Education, 1967).

———— et al., *Health-7: Health, Safety, Fitness* (River Forest, Ill.: Laidlaw, 1966).

Callaghan, J., *Soccer* (Pacific Palisades, Calif.: Goodyear, 1969).

Corbin, C. B., *Becoming Physically Educated in the Elementary School* (Philadelphia, Pa.: Lea and Febiger, 1969).

Dauer, V. P., *Essential Movement Experiences for Preschool and Primary Children* (Minneapolis, Minn.: Burgess, 1972).

———— and R. P. Pangrazi, *Dynamic Physical Education for Elementary School Children* (5th ed.; Minneapolis, Minn.: Burgess, 1975).

Dawson, H. L., *Basic Human Anatomy* (New York: Appleton-Century-Crofts, 1966).

Dexter, G., *The Physical Performance Test for California* (rev.; Sacramento: California State Department of Education, 1971).

Fait, Gregory, and Gerry Fait, *Physical Education for the Elementary School Child* (3rd ed.; Philadelphia, Pa.: W. B. Saunders, 1976).

Fraser, E. D., et al., *The Child and Physical Education* (Englewood Cliffs, N.J.: Prentice-Hall, 1956).

Hall, J. T. *Folk Dance* (Pacific Palisades, Calif.: Goodyear, 1969).

————, *Dance: A Complete Guide to Social, Folk and Square Dancing* (Belmont, Calif.: Wadsworth, 1963).

————, *School Recreation: Its Organization, Supervision and Administration* (Dubuque, Iowa: Wm. C. Brown, 1966).

————, et al., *Fundamentals of Physical Education* (Pacific Palisades, Calif.: Goodyear, 1969).

Holt, J., *How Children Learn* (New York: Pitman, 1967).

Kimber, D. C., et al., *Textbook of Anatomy and Physiology* (New York: Macmillan, 1942).

Latchaw, M., and G. Egstrom, *Human Movement* (Englewood Cliffs, N.J.: Prentice-Hall, 1969).

Lauber, P., *Your Body and How It Works* (New York: Random House, 1962).

Miller, A. G., and V. Whitcomb, *Physical Education in the Elementary School Curriculum* (3rd ed.; Englewood Cliffs, N.J.: Prentice-Hall, 1969).

Neilson, N. P., and W. Van Hagen, *Physical Education for Elementary Schools* (New York: A. S. Barnes, 1954).

Perry, R. H., *Men's Basketball* (Pacific Palisades, Calif.: Goodyear, 1969).

Physical Education Teaching Guide, Grades Three, Four, Five, Six, Division of Instructional Services, Publication No. EC-537 (Los Angeles: Los Angeles City Schools, 1961).

Richardson, H. A., *Games for the Elementary School Grades* (Minneapolis, Minn.: Burgess, 1951).

Safrit, M., *Evaluation in Physical Education: Assessing Motor Behavior* (Englewood Cliffs, N.J.: Prentice-Hall, 1973).

Sandefur, R., *Volleyball* (Pacific Palisades, Calif.: Goodyear, 1970).

Schurr, E. L., *Movement Experiences for Children: Curriculum and Methods for Elementary School Physical Education* (New York: Appleton-Century-Crofts, 1967).

Smith, J. W., et al., *Outdoor Education* (2nd ed.; Englewood Cliffs, N.J.: Prentice-Hall, n.d.).

Stallings, L. M., *Motor Skills, Development and Learning* (Dubuque, Iowa: Wm. C. Brown, 1973).

Stutts, A., *Women's Basketball* (Pacific Palisades, Calif.: Goodyear, 1969).

Vannier, M., and M. Foster, *Teaching Physical Education in Elementary Schools* (Philadelphia, Pa.: W. B. Saunders, 1968).

Wallis, E. L., and G. A. Logan, *Exercise for Children.* (Englewood Cliffs, N.J.: Prentice-Hall, 1966).

Wilson, C. C., and E. A. Wilson, *Health and Living, Teachers' Guide* (New York: Bobbs-Merrill, 1965).

INDEX OF ACTIVITIES AND TERMS

A

Accents, 35
Accident prevention, 213
Adrenal glands, 202
Adrenalin, 202
All-American Promenade, 43
Allemande left, 36
Alternate Toe Touch, 82, 114
Alunelul, 50
Antibodies, 212
Antigens, 212
Anus, 208
Arteries, 198
Asp, 106
Asthma, 204
Atrophy, 194
Auricles, 198

B

Backward Extension Roll, 123
Backward Roll, 96
Bacteria, 200, 212
Balance and Reverse, 86, 115
Balance beam activities, 98, 100, 125
Balance Beam Routine, 125
Balance step, 36
Balance Touch, 83
Balancing activities, 14, 83, 86, 98, 100,
   115, 125
Ball activities, 132, 137, 138, 140, 142,
   143, 146, 150-153, 154-157, 158-160,
   162-164, 166-168
Ball and Stick Relay, 142
Banjo position, 36, 58
Banner, decorative, 186
Base of Support, 118
Basketball, 162-165
Basketball score sheet, 165
Batting, 168
Batting tee, 168
Beanbag activities, 32
Beat, 35
Behavioral skills, 3
Bicycling, 92, 100
Bleking step, 36
Blocking in soccer, 151
Blood, 198

Blood cells
   red, 198
   white, 198, 212
Blood vessels, 198
Body block, 151
Bones. *See also* Skeletal system
   appendicular, 192
   axial, 192
Box Ball, 138
Braille, 206
Brain, 206
Bridge, the, 117
Bronchitis, 204

C

Calcium, 192, 211
Calcium phosphate, 192
Camping, 184
Cancer, 204
Carbohydrates, 210
Carbon dioxide, 204
Cardiovascular recovery, 10
Cardiovascular system, 191, 198-199
Cartwheel, 126
Catching. *See also* Receiving
   in basketball, 162
   in softball, 167
Cell, 189-190, 213
   blood, 198, 212
Center pass, 154
Cerebellum, 206
Cerebrum, 206
Chain Tag, 139
Charley horse, 194
Circles, 101
Clothing, 130-131
Coffee Grinder, 87, 100
Cognition, 3
Cognitive skills, 3, 11
Conation, 3
Continuous Forward Roll, 115
Contraction, 17
Copper, 211
Corner, 36
Crafts, 184-187
Crane, 75, 85
Crane Dive, 85, 115
Crown the King, 140

D

Dance, 35-79
  basic formations, 37-38
  description chart, 41
  evaluation forms, 49, 61, 78
  positions, 39-40
  square, 70
  terms, 36
Deciduous, 183
Diaphragm, 204
Digestion, 208
Digestive system, 191, 208-209
Diseases, 212
  body's defenses against, 212
Dive Roll, 107
Dodge Ball
  individual, 132
  team, 143
Dormant, 183
Do-si-do, 36
Double Clap Polka, 44
Double Forward Roll, 104
Dress-up Relay, 130-131
Dribbling
  in basketball, 163
  in soccer, 152
Duct, 202

E

Education
  four fundamental concepts of, 2-3
  Seven Cardinal Aims of, 2
Emphysema, 204
Endocrine system, 191, 202-203
Enzymes, 208
Equilibrium, 10
Esophagus, 208
Evaluating, 6
Evaluation forms
  for dance, 49, 61, 78
  for stunts and tumbling, 99, 113, 127
Exhale, 204
Exoskeleton, 183, 192
Expansion, 17
Expiration, 204

F

Fabrics, 130-131
Face-to-face, back-to-back step, 36
Falling, 88
Fats, 210
Femur, 192
Fever, 212
Find a Place, 144
Flag Football, 154-157
Flexibility, 10
Forms, 176-181
Forward pass
  receiving, 155
  throwing, 154
Forward Roll, 89-90
  continuous, 115
Forward to Backward Roll, 124
Four Square, 137

G

Gall bladder, 208
Games, 129-147
  "lead-up," 149
Gathering Peasecods, 62-63
Geologist, 133
Germs, 212
Glands
  ductless, 202
  salivary, 208
  sex, 202
Gonads, 202
Grand right and left, 36
Grand Square, 72-73
Grapevine step, 36

H

Handstand
  partner, 108
  spread eagle, 109
Hanging, decorative, 186
Hangman, 135
Haptens, 212
Heading, 151
Headstand
  kick-up, 103
  tripod, 102
Health skills, 10
Heart, 198
Heartbeat, 198
Hindu Tag, 145

Home, 36
Hoop activities, 24
Hopping activities, 18
Hora, 42
Hormones, 202
Hot Time, 70
Human Ball, 91

I

Indoor activities, 133, 135, 144, 185, 186, 187
Inhale, 204
Injury report, 179
Insects, 183, 192
Inside foot, 36
Inside foot trap, 151
Insulin, 202
Inspiration, 204
Instep kick, 150
Insulation, 131
Intensity, 35
Intestine
　large, 208
　small, 208
Invertebrate, 192
Iodine, 211
Iron, 211

J

Jump from Knees, 95
Jump the Shot, 141
Jumping activities, 82, 114, 141
Jumping Jacks, 82, 114

K

Keep Away, 146
Kentwood Schottische, 45
Kicking
　in football, 156
　in soccer, 150
Knee Touch, 84
Kyphosis, 196

L

Lapidary, 133
Larva, 186
Larynx, 204
Leader's self-evaluation checklist, 181

Leadership evaluation, 180
"Lead-up" games, 149
Learning, 3
Lifting activities, 23
Lili Marlene, 53
Liver, 208
Locomotor skills, 4
Longways set, 36
Lordosis, 196
Lummi Stick Dance, 56-57
Lungs, 204
Lymph, 200
Lymph nodes, 200
Lymphatic system, 191, 200-201

M

Making a Straw Horn, 16
Mazurka step, 36, 51-52
Measure, 35
Medulla, 206
Merry-Go-Round, 121
Meter, 35
Microbes, 212
Minerals, 210, 211
Mitosis, 189
Momentum, 95
Monkey Roll, 110
Motivating, 6
Mouth, 208
Movement
　basic, 11
　creative, 13-33
Movement education
　objectives of, 10-11
　principles of, 9-10
Movement skills, 3-4
Muscles
　antagonist, 122, 194
　cardiac, 194
　skeletal, 194
　smooth, 194
　sphincter, 208
　synergist, 122, 194
Muscle cramp, 194
Muscular system, 191, 194-195

N

Nature study, 183-184
Needs, children's
    educational, 2-3
    primary, 1
    secondary, 1-2
Nerves, 206
Nervous system, 191, 206-207
    autonomic, 206
    central, 206
Newspaper Relay, 134
Nose, 204
Nutrition, 210-211
Nuts, nut shells
    crafts items made from, 186, 187
Nutty Animals, 187

O

Old Dobbin, 76-77
One-Arm Wrestle, 122
Organs, 189, 213
    systems of, 191-209, 213
Osmosis, 202
Ossification, 192
Ossified, 192
Osteology, 192
Outside foot, 36
Ovaries, 202
Oxdansen, 54-55
Oxygen, 204

P

Painting, pasta, 185
Pancreas, 202, 208
Papyrus, 133
Parachute activities, 25
Parathyroid, 202
Partner Handstand, 108
Partner Hop, 97
Passing
    in basketball, 162
    in football, 154
Pasta painting, 185
Pattern, 35
Patty-cake Polka, 46
Percentage table, 178

Perspiration, 204
Phosphorus, 211
Phrase, 35
Physical fitness, 10
Pituitary, 202
Place kick, 156
Plasma, 198
Platelets, 198
Pneumonia, 204
Polka, 36, 44, 46, 53
Pollution, air, 204
Posture, 15, 196-197
Potassium, 211
Promenade, 36
Prone, 117
Protein, 192, 210
Protozoa, 212
Punt, 155
    kicking, 156
    receiving, 155
Pupa, 186
Push and Clap, 120
Put Your Little Foot, 51-52

R

Receiving, 155
Record sources, 79
Rectum, 208
Reflex action, 206
Relaxing activities, 33
Relay races, 83, 130-131, 134, 142, 147
Reproductive system, 191
Rescue Relay, 147
Respiration, 204
Respiratory system, 191, 204-205
Rhythm, elements of, 35
Rock
    igneous, 133
    metamorphic, 133
    sedimentary, 133
Rock, Paper, Scissors, 133
Roll
    backward, 96
    backward extension, 123
    continuous forward, 115
    dive, 107
    double forward, 104
    forward, 89-90
    forward to backward, 124
    monkey, 110

Rooster Fight, 112
Rope activities, 26, 27, 28, 29, 30-31
Running
    in football, 156
    in place, 101, 114
Running activities, 17, 101, 114, 134, 136,
    144, 145, 147
Russian Dance, 105, 116
Rye Waltz, 69

S
Safety, 213
Saliva, 208
Salivary glands, 208
Schottische, 36, 45, 59-60
Scoliosis, 196
Score sheets
    for basketball, 165
    for softball, 169
    for track and field, 177
    for volleyball, 161
Scottish Sword Dance, 59-60
Self-actualization, 2
Sensometer, 206
Serving in volleyball, 158, 160
Sex glands, 202
Shell boat, 186
Shooting in basketball, 163
"Shots," 212
Shoulder-waist position, 40
Sidecar position, 36, 58
Six-Legged Animal, 111
Skaters' position, 39
Skeletal system, 191, 192-193
Skills
    behavioral, 3
    cognitive, 3, 11
    emotional, 10-11
    health, 10
    locomotor, 4
    movement, 3-4
    social, 10
Skill drills
    for basketball, 164
    for football, 157
    for soccer, 152-153
    for softball, 168
    for volleyball, 160

Skin the Snake, 106
Skipping activities, 19
Snakes, 106
Soccer, 150-153
Social dance position, 40, 58
Social skills, 10
Sodium, 211
Softball, 166-169
Softball score sheet, 169
Sole-of-foot trap, 151
Spinal cord, 206
Spread Eagle Handstand, 109
Square dances, 70, 71, 72-73
Stability, 118
Stamina, 10
Step close, 36
Sternum, 196
Stimulating, 6
Stomach, 208
Stoop and Stretch, 83
Straw Horn, Making a, 16
Streets and Alleys, 136
Strength, 10
Stretching activities, 20
Stunts, 81-127
Supine, 117
Swinging activities, 22
Symmetry, 98
Systems of organs, 191-209, 213

T
Tag, 136, 139, 145
Taste buds, 208
Tea for Two, 66
Team Dodge Ball, 143
Team sports, 149-181
Temperature elevation, 212
Tempo, 35
Testes, 202
Testing, 6
Teton Mountain Stomp, 58
Throwing in softball, 166
Thyroid, 202
Tikling bird, 75
Time signature, 35
Tinikling, 74-75
Tissues, 213
    connective, 189
    epithelial, 189
    muscle, 189
    nervous, 189

Toe-heel step, 36
Tongue, 208
Torso Twist, 84, 114
Tournaments, 170-175
    elimination, 170, 174
    elimination-consolation, 171
    ladder, 170, 172
    pyramid, 170, 173
    round robin, 171, 175
Trachea, 204
Trapping, 151
Treadmill, 101
Trees, 134, 183
Tripod Headstand, 102
Tripod Tip-up, 94
Tuberculosis, 204
Tumbling, 81-127
Turning activities, 22
Turnover, 119
Twisting activities, 21
Two-step, 36, 64-65, 66

U
Up and Over, 93

V
Vaccination, 212
Varsouvienne, 52
Varsouvienne position, 40
Veins, 198
Ventricles, 198
Vertebrate, 192
Virginia Reel, 47-48
Viruses, 212
Vitamins, 210, 211
Volley
    overhand, 159
    underhand, 159
Volleyball, 158-161
Volleyball score sheet, 161

W
Walking activities, 15
Waltz, 69
    box, 36, 68
    box turn, 68
    progressive, 36, 67
Warm-up activities, 82-84, 100-101,
    114-116
Weathering, 17

INDEX OF SKILLS

Agility, 88, 89-90, 91, 97, 120, 121, 122.
  See also Flexibility
Balance, 14, 83, 84, 85, 86, 87, 92, 93, 94,
  97, 98, 101, 102, 103, 108, 109, 111,
  112, 115, 117, 118, 119, 120, 121, 122,
  124, 125
Balance step, 43, 110
Ball handling, 132, 137, 138, 140, 142,
  143, 146, 150-153, 154-157, 158-160,
  162-164, 166-168
Batting, 168
Bleking step, 36
Blocking, 140
  in soccer, 151
Catching, 162, 167
Conditioning, general, 89-90, 92, 93
Coordination, 102, 103, 104, 105, 106,
  107, 108, 109, 110, 111, 112, 123, 124,
  125, 126
Dance, 42, 43, 44, 45, 46, 47-48, 50,
  51-52, 53, 54-55, 56-57, 58, 59-60,
  62-63, 64-65, 66, 67-68, 69, 70, 72-73,
  74-75, 76-77
Dodging, 136, 139, 143
Dribbling, 152, 163
Flexibility, 85, 92, 93, 94, 95, 106, 107
Grand right and left, 36
Hopping, 74-75, 97
Imaginative skills, 18, 23
Heel-toe step, 46
Hopping, 18
Jumping, 82, 114, 141
Kicking, 150, 156
Manipulative skills, 24, 25, 26, 27, 28, 29,
  30-31, 32
Mazurka step, 36, 51-52
Movement, basic, 14, 15, 17, 18, 19, 20,
  22, 23

Movement sequence, remembering, 125
Passing, 154, 162
Polka step, 36, 44, 46, 53
Receiving, 155
Reel, 47-48
Relaxing, 33
Remembering movement sequence, 125
Rhythmic skills, 26. *See also* Dance
Roll lead-up skills, 88
Rolling, 89-90, 96, 104, 107, 110, 115,
  123, 124
Running, 17, 101, 130, 134, 136, 138, 139,
  144, 145, 147, 156
Schottische step, 36, 45, 59-60
Serving, 158
Shooting in basketball, 163
Shuffle walk, 76-77
Side step, 42, 50
Skipping, 19, 47-48
Sliding, 46, 53, 62-63
Spatial awareness, 88, 89-90, 91
Springing, 54-55
Stamping, 50, 54-55
Step-hop, 42
Strength, 85, 86, 87, 92, 93, 94, 95, 102,
  103, 104, 105, 108, 109, 117, 118, 119,
  123, 126
Stretching, 20
Team spirit, 130, 134, 142, 146
Throwing, 138, 166
Timing, 110, 111, 112
Trapping, 151
Twisting, 21
Two-step, 36, 64-65, 66
Walking, 15, 43, 47, 58, 62-63, 69, 70,
  72-73
Waltz step, 36, 67, 68, 69